**SCHOLASTIC**

# Differentiated Activities
# for Teaching Key
# Comprehension Skills

**40+** Ready-to-Go Reproducibles
That Help Students at Different Skill
Levels All Meet the Same Standards

**Martin Lee and Marcia Miller**

New York • Toronto • London • Auckland • Sydney
Mexico City • New Delhi • Hong Kong • Buenos Aires

**Teaching** *Resources*

Our sincere thanks go to Sarah Longhi for her clarity,
guidance, and dedication to this project.

Photo Credits: Page 47 © Defense Department, Marine Corps; Page 48 © Joe Rosenthal/
Associated Press; Page 53 © The Granger Collection; Page 59 © Cynthia Johnson/Gettyimages;
Page 60 © Associated Press

Poetry Credits: Page 65: "October" by Winifred C. Marshall and "Green-Apple Morning" by Mary
Graham Bond are reprinted from POETRY PLACE ANTHOLOGY. Copyright © 1983 by Edgell
Communications by permission of Scholastic Inc.

Editor: Sarah Longhi
Content editor: Nicole Iorio
Designer: Holly Grundon
Illustrator: Mike Moran
Cover designer: Maria Lilja

ISBN-13: 978-0-545-23451-1
ISBN-10: 0-545-23451-4

# Contents

# Activities

# Introduction

Each child arrives in your classroom with a unique set of experiences, abilities, and needs. Prior knowledge, language skill, ability to focus, and other key factors vary widely in any grouping.

Given the challenge of helping all learners master core grade-level concepts and skills, how can you address a typical range of needs without creating 30 different plans per lesson per subject per day? You can differentiate your instruction, adjusting your presentation style and modifying the level of challenge for learners at several levels rather than expecting students to adapt themselves to a standard curriculum or method of teaching (Hall, 2002).

This book can be an effective tool to help you differentiate reading instruction. Each lesson opens with a passage for all students to read. (Passage selections include both fiction and nonfiction pieces that vary in genre and style.) After the passage, you'll find three leveled activity sheets, each offering comprehension and word-study questions that target important reading skills and strategies. As they complete their tiered activities, students move along different but related paths to actively process information and demonstrate learning. They read, think, respond, summarize, retell, write, explain, extrapolate, and create projects.

The chart below summarizes the key elements of differentiated instruction. We use the acronym *CAP,* for Content, Approach, and Product. Teachers *plan CAP*; students *perform CAP.* For each tier, notice what the teacher does and what students do.

| TEACHERS | "CAP" | STUDENTS |
|---|---|---|
| Select materials<br>Set goals<br>Prepare lessons | **CONTENT**<br>*Consistent for all* | Choose materials<br>Understand objectives<br>Clarify expectations |
| Make groupings<br>Address modalities<br>Vary pacing<br>Provide support | **APPROACH**<br>*Differentiate as needed* | Get involved<br>Apply skills<br>Develop strategies<br>Sharpen techniques |
| Develop activities<br>Make adjustments<br>Wrap up the experience<br>Extend | **PRODUCT**<br>*Ideal for differentiation* | Present projects<br>Participate in discussion<br>Perform assessment<br>Reflect on learning |

Differentiated instruction isn't a single strategy. Rather, this flexible and research-based approach incorporates many strategies to better serve student diversity. In *Integrating Differentiated Instruction and Understanding by Design*, Carol Ann Tomlinson and Jay McTighe state that differentiated instruction "… focuses on whom we teach, where we teach, and how we teach" (2006).

# Using This Book

In developing this book, we have used the *CAP* model as a structural guideline to streamline your efforts to differentiate instruction. We hope the lessons will serve as tools to empower you to become more familiar and comfortable with implementing tiered activities.

Here is how we suggest you use this book:

Each lesson begins with *content* that is consistent for all students, in the form of a short reading passage. We have selected topics and genres that support the goals and tasks described on the teacher page. In previewing, reading, and discussing the reading passage with the whole class, you guide students to clarify objectives and expectations.

Our *approach* is to have students complete one of the three leveled activity sheets developed for that reading passage. Each level is identified throughout the book by its own recurring icon.

◆ Tier 1 is best used with struggling learners.

● Tier 2 is intended for use with students who are performing on level.

⬠ Tier 3 is designed to challenge more advanced students.

As students work through the activity sheets individually, in pairs, or in small groups, they interact with the passage, applying skills, developing strategies, and sharpening their techniques for completing the tasks. The accompanying teacher page offers ideas to guide you as you prepare the lesson. It suggests how to encourage and support students in each tier. Each activity sheet also presents Word Work, a word-study activity designed to help students attend to word parts, word patterns, and grammatical structure as they read.

The *product* for each lesson is a blend of the written responses to questions, the Word Work tasks, and the response to a multiple-choice item about the passage. It might also include one or more of the reading response activities at the back of the book, as well as students' participation in discussion and their reflections on their work. We hope that the selections themselves inspire you to add your own ideas so that you can further engage your students as they extend their learning.

Keep in mind that the key to successful differentiated instruction is to know your students.

❖ Observe early and often to determine *how* to differentiate, and whether the approaches you've presented are working.

## Each Lesson Includes:

**TEACHER PAGE**

**DATA PAGE**

**TIER 1 PAGE**

**TIER 2 PAGE**

**TIER 3 PAGE**

## Sources:

Gregory, G. H. & Chapman, C. (2002). *Differentiated instructional strategies: One size doesn't fit all.* Thousand Oaks, CA: Corwin Press.

Hall, T. (2002). Differentiated instruction. Wakefield, MA: National Center on Accessing the General Curriculum. Retrieved from http://www.cast.org/publications/ncac/ncac_diffinstruc.html

Heacox, D. (2002). *Differentiating instruction in the regular classroom: How to reach and teach all learners, grades 3–12.* Minneapolis, MN: Free Spirit Publications.

Tomlinson, C. A. & McTighe, J. (2006). *Integrating differentiated instruction & understanding by design.* Alexandria, VA: Association for Supervision and Curriculum Development.

❖ Be flexible! Adjust and adapt grouping, pacing, modalities, and support as needed.

❖ Encourage and model active reading. Suggest that students jot down ideas on sticky notes, circle or underline hard words, sketch scenes for clarity and visualization, or take margin notes. To support struggling readers, echo-read some passages, or record the passages so they can listen and follow along in the text. Model techniques to unlock new vocabulary.

❖ Mix and match tasks, presentations, or activities within tiers to better fit your students' abilities and interests.

❖ Help students make good choices that can propel their learning. For example, suggest that struggling writers use graphic organizers, highlighter pens, or peer-partner chats. Advanced learners might debate solutions, research additional data, or pursue tangential ideas.

❖ Expect students to demonstrate learning at their own level. Ideally, differentiated instruction should provide ample challenge to stimulate students to work and succeed, but not so much as to cause them stress or lead them to a point of frustration.

❖ Provide feedback as often as possible while students work; invite them to express their thinking or explain their solution strategies.

❖ Encourage self-assessment to empower students to identify their own strengths and weaknesses. This can lead students to deeper ownership of their responsibilities as learners.

## Reading Standards Correlation Grid

Although there are varied standards to guide reading comprehension instruction, we present here a streamlined version to identify which major skills have been addressed in each lesson. The lessons align with the Standards for the English Language Arts created by the International Reading Association and the National Council of Teacher of English (see www.reading.org), with focus on the following:

❖ Students read a wide range of print and nonprint texts to build an understanding of texts, of themselves, and of the cultures of the United States and the world; to acquire new information; to respond to the needs and demands of society and the workplace; and for personal fulfillment. Among these texts are fiction and nonfiction, classic, and contemporary works.

❖ Students apply a wide range of strategies to comprehend, interpret, evaluate, and appreciate texts. They draw on their prior experience, their interactions with other readers and writers, their knowledge of word meaning and of other texts, their word identification strategies, and their understanding of textual features (e.g., sound-letter correspondence, sentence structure, context graphics).

We have also aligned our lessons to the McREL Content Knowledge standards for language arts (see www.mcrel.org/compendium) and the overarching reading standards:

❖ Uses the general skills and strategies of the reading process

❖ Uses reading skills and strategies to understand and interpret a variety of literary texts

❖ Uses reading skills and strategies to understand and interpret a variety of informational texts

| | Set a Purpose for Reading | Recognize Author's Purpose/Point of View | Understand Literary Elements | Identify Main Idea and Supporting Details | Analyze Text Elements and Structures | Compare and Contrast | Recognize Cause and Effect | Differentiate Between Fact and Opinion | Identify Symbolism and Figurative Language | Summarize | Make Connections | Draw Conclusions/Infer |
|---|---|---|---|---|---|---|---|---|---|---|---|---|
| 1. How to Train a Puppy Not to Jump | ✔ | | | ✔ | ✔ | | ✔ | | | ✔ | ✔ | |
| 2. Freddy's E-Mail | | ✔ | ✔ | ✔ | ✔ | | ✔ | ✔ | | | | ✔ |
| 3. A Family Movie Classic | ✔ | ✔ | ✔ | ✔ | ✔ | ✔ | | | | ✔ | ✔ | |
| 4. Is That You, Jack? | | ✔ | ✔ | ✔ | | ✔ | ✔ | | | ✔ | | ✔ |
| 5. Shades of Meaning | ✔ | | | ✔ | | ✔ | ✔ | ✔ | | | ✔ | |
| 6. Two Rice Cakes | | | ✔ | ✔ | | ✔ | ✔ | | ✔ | | ✔ | ✔ |
| 7. School-Schedule Debate | ✔ | ✔ | | ✔ | ✔ | ✔ | ✔ | | | ✔ | ✔ | ✔ |
| 8. The Navajo Code Talkers | ✔ | ✔ | | ✔ | | ✔ | ✔ | ✔ | | | | ✔ |
| 9. Eye-Witness to History | | ✔ | ✔ | ✔ | | ✔ | ✔ | | | ✔ | ✔ | ✔ |
| 10. Amazing Grace, Computer Ace | ✔ | ✔ | | ✔ | | ✔ | ✔ | | ✔ | ✔ | | |
| 11. Two Poems | | ✔ | | ✔ | ✔ | ✔ | | | ✔ | | ✔ | ✔ |
| 12. Gliding Through the Air | | ✔ | ✔ | ✔ | ✔ | ✔ | ✔ | ✔ | | ✔ | ✔ | ✔ |

# Teaching **How to Train a Puppy Not to Jump**

**Skills:**
- Setting a purpose for reading nonfiction
- Recognizing cause and effect
- Drawing conclusions

Students read a set of instructions for training a puppy.

| Tasks | Tier 1<br>Below Level | Tier 2<br>On Level | Tier 3<br>Above Level |
|---|:---:|:---:|:---:|
| Set a purpose for reading nonfiction | X | X | X |
| Use text features (bulleted and numbered lists) | X | X | X |
| Recognize cause and effect | X | X | X |
| Draw conclusions | | | X |
| Recognize words that contain silent letters | X | | |
| Use synonyms | | X | X |

## Getting Started

See the tips below for introducing the lesson. Make copies of the reading passage (pages 9–10) and the appropriate leveled activity sheet for each group of learners (pages 11–13).

Access prior knowledge by discussing what students know about caring for and training pets. Remind students of cause-and-effect relationships that appear in the text. Also talk about how bulleted and numbered lists can help readers understand a how-to article.

 **Tier 1**

- **Purpose for Reading/Use Text Features:** Have students use the title to predict what the passage will be about. Then answer items 1–3 together.

- **Cause and Effect** Discuss that each step is meant to change the dog's behavior. Talk about items 4 and 5, focusing on the cause and effect in each.

- **Word Work:** Silent letters can be challenging for English language learners. Model correct pronunciations to help students recognize the silent letters. Provide additional examples.

 **Tier 2**

- **Purpose for Reading/Use Text Features:** Talk about ways to guide reading, such as using a title to predict content. Answer item 1 together.

- **Cause and Effect:** Discuss items 2 and 3, focusing on the cause-and-effect relationships.

- **Word Work:** Discuss that synonyms have *nearly* the same meaning. Guide students to choose synonyms that best match the word's meaning as it appears in context in the text.

 **Tier 3**

- **Purpose for Reading/Use Text Features:** Have students identify the helpful text features in the article. Talk about why numbering training steps is more useful than bulleting them.

- **Cause and Effect:** Discuss item 3, focusing on the cause-and-effect relationships of each action.

- **Draw Conclusions:** Have students share their answers to item 4. Discuss that different dog trainers may draw different conclusions about the causes of dog behaviors.

- **Word Work:** Invite small groups to brainstorm other synonyms for each given word.

**Skills:**
- Setting a purpose for reading nonfiction
- Recognizing cause and effect
- Drawing conclusions

# How to Train a Puppy Not to Jump: Reading Passage

Most dog owners agree that it's not wise to allow their dogs to jump on people and things. A friendly puppy that jumps can cause trouble without meaning any harm. It can hurt someone or leave unwanted scratches on something. A puppy's claws can rip clothing and muddy paws can leave dirty prints. A jumping puppy can also frighten a small child. The puppy might even knock the child down, leading to an injury. This is not how you want your dog to behave!

Puppies want to be with people. If you remove the puppy immediately when he does something wrong, he'll soon get the message. He'll stop jumping! Here is one way to teach a puppy not to jump up. Use these tips for training.

### What You'll Need

- your puppy

- a collar and leash

- a calm person to act as a guest

- a room with a door

# How to Train a Puppy Not to Jump
### (continued)

## Follow these steps when your puppy jumps on your guest:

**1.** Calmly and quietly take the puppy on leash to another room. Do not yell or hit. Don't jerk the leash.

**2.** Stay there with the pup. Wait for 5 seconds in silence. Then bring the dog back near the guest.

**3.** If your pup jumps again, take it right back to the other room on a leash. Wait 5 seconds before bringing it back near your guest.

**4.** If your pup jumps a third time, lead it to the other room once more. Now leave it there *alone* for 10 seconds. Think of this as a puppy "time out."

**5.** Go back for your puppy. Bring it to your guest. Repeat as needed until your dog doesn't jump.

## How your guests can help:

**A.** Ask your guests to knock before entering.

**B.** Tell guests not to push your dog off when he jumps on them. That's because pushing means, "What fun! Let's do it again!" in dog language. Instead, tell your guest to simply turn away from the dog. To a dog, this means, "Stop. I don't want to play with you now."

 *Differentiated Activities for Teaching Key Comprehension Skills: Grades 4–6* © 2010 by Martin Lee and Marcia Miller. Scholastic Teaching Resources

# How to Train a Puppy Not to Jump: Activity Sheet

**( Read and Understand )** Read the passage. Then answer the questions.

**1.** Read the title and the first paragraph. What problem will this article help you solve?

_____

**2.** Why are the training steps numbered? _____

**3.** Which steps tell you what to do when the puppy jumps on a person the first time?

_____

**4.** Suppose you push away your jumping puppy. What does the puppy think you mean?

_____

_____

**( Word Work: Silent Letters )**

The words *frighten*, *knock*, *guest*, *calmly* and *wrong* are in the how-to article.
Each word has one or two silent letters.

  fri**gh**ten      **k**nock      ca**l**mly      g**u**est      **w**rong

Read aloud each word. Circle the words with silent letters. Underline all silent letters.

| light | path  | ghost | know   |
|-------|-------|-------|--------|
| very  | knit  | talk  | scene  |
| dish  | sign  | fresh | thumb  |
| two   | guard | ring  | island |

**( Check )** Circle the best choice.

**What can your guests do to help train your puppy not to jump up?**

A. Gently push the puppy away.          C. Turn away from the puppy.

B. Leave the room.                      D. Say, "Time out!"

# How to Train a Puppy
# Not to Jump: Activity Sheet

**Read and Understand**   Read the passage. Then answer the questions.

**1.** What do you want to find out by reading this piece? _____

_____

**2.** Read the bulleted list that shows what you need to train a puppy. Why do you think

the guest needs to be calm? _____

_____

**3.** Why are the training steps numbered? _____

**4.** What words are most important to follow in section B? _____

**Word Work: Synonyms**

*Synonyms* are words that have the same or similar meanings. Each word in the left column appears in the how-to article. Find the word in the article. Then write a synonym for it.

| Word From Passage | Synonym |
|---|---|
| wise | |
| frighten | |
| guest | |
| hit | |
| simply | |

**Check**   Circle the best choice.

**What is different about the puppy's training the third time it jumps?**

A. The pup is not removed to another room.

B. The pup stays alone in the other room and for twice as long.

C. The pup goes into the other room, but off-leash this time.

D. The pup stops jumping after it.

# How to Train a Puppy Not to Jump: Activity Sheet

**Read and Understand** ) Read the passage. Then answer the questions.

**1.** What do you expect to learn by reading this piece? _____

_____

**2.** How does the author use text features to explain the training? _____

_____

**3.** What effect does pushing the puppy off cause? Explain. _____

_____

**4.** How often should you remove a dog from a room when it misbehaves? _____

**Word Work: Synonyms** )

*Synonyms* are words that have the same or similar meanings. Words in the left column are from the how-to article. The right column has synonyms for each word. Complete the table.

| Word From Passage | Synonym |
|---|---|
| wise | |
| | remain |
| guest | |
| | scare |
| | promptly |

**Check** ) Circle the best choice.

## What is different about the puppy's training the third time it jumps?

A. The pup is removed to another room.

B. The pup stays alone in the other room and for twice as long.

C. The pup goes into the other room off-leash.

D. The pup stops jumping after it.

# Teaching
# Freddy's E-Mail

**Skill:**

Identifying main idea and details

Making inferences

Students read an e-mail written from an older brother to a younger brother; they identify main ideas and make inferences.

| Tasks | Tier 1 Below Level | Tier 2 On Level | Tier 3 Above Level |
|---|---|---|---|
| Identify main idea and details | X | X | X |
| Develop vocabulary | X | X | X |
| Make inferences | | X | X |
| Use multiple-meaning words | X | X | |
| Understand hyphenated words | | | X |

## Getting Started

See the tips below for introducing the lesson. Make copies of the passage (page 15) and the appropriate leveled activity sheet for each group of learners (pages 16–18). Access prior knowledge and build background on these topics from the passage: field trips, e-mail structure, and community service.

 **Tier 1**

- **Identify Main Idea:** Have students briefly summarize Freddy's experience. Then answer Item 1 together, with students suggesting alternate subject lines.

- **Develop Vocabulary:** Direct students to the first paragraph of the e-mail to find the target word they use in item 2.

- **Find Supporting Details:** Suggest that partners reread parts of the e-mail to each other to help answer items 3 and 4.

- **Word Work:** Model using context clues to pick the applicable meaning for the given usage of a multiple-meaning word. Brainstorm with students to list other multiple-meaning words they frequently encounter.

 **Tier 2**

- **Make Inferences:** Review the strategy of *inferring* as making "educated guesses by reading between the lines." Suggest that students imagine themselves as the "I" (Freddy) and have them infer how Freddy and Squirt are related, noting textual clues that support their ideas. Then have them answer items 1 and 2.

- **Develop Vocabulary:** Direct students to paragraph 3 of the e-mail to locate the target synonym in item 3.

- **Identify Main Idea:** For items 4 and 5, have students express the main idea of each paragraph, as well as the main idea of the entire e-mail. Ask them to identify supporting details, and to distinguish key details from extra information.

- **Word Work:** Model using context clues to pick the applicable meaning for each multiple-meaning word. Brainstorm with students to list other multiple-meaning words they frequently encounter.

 **Tier 3**

- **Identify Main Idea/Make Inferences:** Review the first two bulleted tips for on-level learners. Then have students answer items 1–3.

- **Develop Vocabulary:** Direct students to paragraph 3 of the e-mail to locate the target synonym in item 5. Challenge students to infer how the dog run's *storage sheds* might be used.

- **Word Work:** Review that hyphenated words act together to express a single thought. Point out that the hyphenated words in this passage appear *before* the words they describe. Provide other examples students can examine, including numbers written in word form (e.g., fifty-two, one-third).

Name _____ Date _____

# Freddy's E-Mail:
## Reading Passage

New    Reply    Forward    Send/Receive    Delete

| To: | jbrow2002@mail.usa |
| --- | --- |
| From: | fbrow1996@mail.usa |
| Date: | April 23, 2010 |
| Subject: | Field trip update |

Hi, Squirt!

What a great field trip—and with overnights, too! Our class is doing a community service project. We're helping to turn a vacant lot into a dog run. I bet you don't even know what a dog run is. It's a fenced-in area where dogs play off-leash—like a doggy playground.

Dr. Chen, a local vet, came up with the idea. She believes that city dogs need to be able to run free in a safe space. I guess that dog owners and city leaders agreed with her.

The project has been going on for weeks. Many people and groups are helping. A fence company donated and installed a chain-link fence to enclose the space. It has a two-gate entrance that helps keep frisky dogs from escaping as people come and go. My teacher had us find the perimeter of the dog run. We measured the length of the sides with dog leashes!

Last night, a lumber yard delivered a giant load of wood chips. It was our class's job to turn them into a natural "carpet" for the dogs. First, we raked the ground clean and smooth. Then we spread out the wood chips evenly everywhere. It was hard, sweaty labor. Snacks and a lunch break really kept us going. So did the loud music the plumbing crew blasted as they installed the water pipes.

Tomorrow, after breakfast, my team will sand wooden benches. Another team will paint storage sheds. A third team will install hooks where owners can hang dog leashes. After all that hard work, we'll have a cookout to celebrate our teamwork and the finished dog run.

I'm not sure when the dog run officially opens. But when it does, let's bring Sparky. Our pooch will love digging and racing around with his dog buddies.

See you Friday night. Say hi to Mom and Dad. They knew that I thought this was going to be a stupid trip. But tell them I've changed my mind. It's actually fun to get dirty AND make a difference. And get some time away from you, Squirt!

Love,
Freddy

#  Freddy's E-Mail: Activity Sheet

**Read and Understand**  Read the passage. Then answer the questions.

**1.** How is an e-mail's subject line like a main idea? _____

**2.** What describing word in Paragraph 1 means *empty* or *unused?* _____

**3.** What was Dr. Chen's part in this project? _____

**4.** What details show how Freddy's class is helping to build the dog run? Put a star beside the details.

**5.** What is the main idea of Paragraph 4? _____

_____

**Word Work: Multiple-Meaning Words**

Use clues from the passage and your own word knowledge to fill in the chart.

| Word | Meaning in This Passage | Other Meanings |
|------|-------------------------|----------------|
| **trip** | journey, outing | stumble |
| **space** | | |
| **fence** | | |

**Check**  Circle the best choice.

## How will Freddy's class celebrate doing their part of the project?

A. with a cookout

B. by adopting a class pet

C. with a field trip to Dr. Chen's office

D. by planning a dog show in the new dog run

Name _____          Date _____

 # Freddy's E-Mail: Activity Sheet

**Read and Understand** ) Read the passage. Then answer the questions.

**1.** How are Freddy and Squirt related? _____

Put a star next to the clues that help you know.

**2.** What could Freddy's reason be for writing? _____

**3.** Which word is a synonym for *gave for free*? _____

**4.** What is the main idea of paragraph 5? _____

**5.** What other subject line might fit this e-mail? _____

**Word Work: Multiple-Meaning Words** )

Use clues from the passage and your own word knowledge to fill in the chart.

| Word | Meaning in This Passage | Other Meanings |
|------|------------------------|----------------|
| **trip** | journey, outing | |
| **space** | | |
| **fence** | | |
| **sheds** | | |

**Check** ) Circle the best choice.

**How did Freddy's teacher bring math into the field trip?**

A. Students weighed the wood chips.

B. Students counted the money that was donated.

C. Students practiced number facts as they worked.

D. Students measured and estimated the perimeter of the dog run.

# Freddy's E-Mail: Activity Sheet

**Read and Understand**  Read the passage. Then answer the questions.

**1.** In your own words, state the main idea of this e-mail. _____

_____

**2.** What is Freddy's role in the project? _____

**3.** What benefits might dog owners get? _____

**4.** What details support the idea that city leaders agreed with Dr. Chen? _____

_____

**5.** Which word from the selection might describe dogs that *romp*? _____

**Word Work: Hyphenated Words**

A *hyphen* (–) can connect two words to form a new word. Hyphenated words are often used to describe. Using four hyphenated words from the e-mail, complete the table.

| Hyphenated Word | Meaning |
|---|---|
| | |
| | |
| | |
| | |

**Check**  Circle the best choice.

**How did Freddy's teacher bring math into the field trip?**

A.  Students weighed the wood chips.

B.  Students counted the money that was donated.

C.  Students practiced number facts as they worked.

D.  Students measured and estimated the perimeter of the dog run.

# Teaching **A Family Classic**

Students examine elements of a review of the movie *The Wizard of Oz*.

**Skills:**
- Distinguishing fact from opinion
- Determining author's point of view

| Tasks | ◆ Tier 1 Below Level | ● Tier 2 On Level | ⬟ Tier 3 Above Level |
|---|:---:|:---:|:---:|
| Distinguish fact from opinion | X | X | X |
| Determine author's point of view | X | X | X |
| Understand direct quotations | | X | X |
| Analyze compound words | X | X | |
| Select synonyms and antonyms | | | X |

## Getting Started

See the tips below for introducing the lesson. Make copies of the reading passage (page 20) and the appropriate leveled activity sheet for each group of learners (pages 21–23).

Access prior knowledge of *The Wizard of Oz* and discuss what students know about versions of books, films, cartoons, music, and toys related to it. Talk about the elements of a review.

 ## Tier 1

- **Fact and Opinion:** Explain that a fact is a piece of information that can be proven while an opinion is an attitude or belief based on someone's personal views. Facts are either true or false, while opinions are neither right nor wrong. Provide realistic examples of facts and opinions for students to classify. Then help students answer items 1 and 2.

- **Point of View:** Define point of view as a person's way of thinking and point out that knowing an author's point of view helps us better evaluate that reasoning in the passage. Guide students to answer items 3 and 4.

- **Word Work:** Present these familiar compound words for students to read and separate into parts: *sunlight, homework, bookmark*. Then have individuals complete this section.

 ## Tier 2

- **Fact and Opinion:** Review that a fact is a statement that can be proven and an opinion is a personal belief. Facts are either true or false; opinions are neither right nor wrong. Guide students to separate facts from opinions to answer items 1 and 2.

- **Quotation Marks:** Draw attention to words in the review that appear inside quotation marks. Clarify what these marks mean, and how knowing this helps students answer item 3.

- **Point of View:** Tell students that anytime someone writes a review, we are reading an opinion. Good reviews also include facts to help readers make up their own minds. Have students locate text support for the reviewer's point of view as they answer item 4.

- **Word Work:** Brainstorm and list familiar compound words students can separate into their parts. Then have them complete this section.

 ## Tier 3

- **Fact and Opinion:** Ask students to define what a fact and an opinion are. Then have them suggest examples of each.

- **Point of View:** Discuss how reviewers' own preferences influence their evaluations of a film.

- **Text Features:** For item 4, explain different ways a reviewer might highlight key facts: by using quotation marks, italics, or other text features, such as bold type or underlining.

- **Word Work:** Distinguish between synonyms and antonyms by brainstorming some of each for these words from the review: *scary, laugh, old-fashioned*. Then have individuals complete this section.

**Skills:**
- Distinguishing fact from opinion
- Determining author's point of view

# A Family Movie Classic:
## Reading Passage

I like movies to be funny and scary. Add some action, lively music, a cute animal, a hero, and a happy ending, and I am hooked. This is why I love *The Wizard of Oz*. It came out in 1939, but I bet it is as exciting to new audiences today as it was back then.

Most people are familiar with Dorothy and the tornado that takes her away. Many of us first saw *The Wizard of Oz* with our parents and fondly recall this experience. It is the perfect movie for families to watch together.

This great film starts in black and white. It may look old-fashioned, but this start is important since we first meet Dorothy, her dog, and all the members of her family's farm. Nobody in Kansas has time for Dorothy, and this is when she sings "Over the Rainbow" to express how lonely she feels. She daydreams about a happier place to live.

Parts of *The Wizard of Oz* are scary, but they are not like a horror film. Dorothy and Toto get trapped in the old farmhouse. They spin, bounce, and fly through the sky. When the farmhouse lands, Dorothy's adventures can *really* start. She opens the door—and steps into a new world, filled with bright colors.

Many surprises await Dorothy as she and her friends "follow the yellow brick road." The more I see this film, the more I take in. Jokes I missed at first now give me a good laugh. I notice clever details in the sets. I now know many of the lines by heart. Even the soundtrack fits just right! It actually won for the best music in a movie that year.

I do feel that the acting, special effects, and dialogue are corny, but they still work. I love the cast, who act, sing, dance, and bring the story to life. If you ask people to name a favorite character or scene from *The Wizard of Oz*, you will get many answers. The film is so amazing because it has something for everyone.

I've seen *The Wizard of Oz* only on TV. Someday I hope to see it in on the big screen of a movie theater. I want to see it as the audiences did so long ago. *The Wizard of Oz* is like a favorite stuffed toy. It may be old, but it is dearly loved and comforting. I give this classic film five stars!

*Differentiated Activities for Teaching Key Comprehension Skills: Grades 4–6* © 2010 by Martin Lee and Marcia Miller. Scholastic Teaching Resources

# A Family Movie Classic: Activity Sheet

**Read and Understand**) Read the passage. Then answer the questions.

**1.** The reviewer gives *The Wizard of Oz* five stars. Circle five comments in the review that support this top rating.

**2.** List two facts the reviewer gives about *The Wizard of Oz.* _____

_____

**3.** How does the reviewer feel about the film's scary parts? _____

_____

**4.** What is the reviewer's opinion of the special effects? _____

_____

**Word Work: Compound Words**)

A *compound word* is made of two separate words that become a new word when joined. **Farmhouse** is made up of **farm + house**. Find four more compound words in the passage to add to the chart.

| Compound Word | Separate Words |
|---|---|
| farmhouse | farm **+** house |
|  | + |
|  | + |
|  | + |
|  | + |

**Check**) Circle the best choice.

## Which of the following is an opinion?

A. *The Wizard of Oz* starts slowly.

B. *The Wizard of Oz* came out in 1939.

C. Dorothy sings "Over the Rainbow."

D. This film starts in black and white.

# A Family Movie Classic: Activity Sheet

**Read and Understand**  Read the passage. Then answer the questions.

**1.** List two facts the reviewer includes about *The Wizard of Oz.* _____

_____

**2.** List two opinions the reviewer has about *The Wizard of Oz.* _____

_____

**3.** Why does "follow the yellow brick road" have quotation marks? _____

_____

**4.** What details support the claim that *The Wizard of Oz* has something for everyone?

_____

**Word Work: Compound Words**

A *compound* word is made of two separate words put together as one. **Something** comes from **some + thing**. It means any object. Write 5 more compound words from the passage.

| Compound Word | Separate Words | Meaning |
|---|---|---|
|  | + |  |
|  | + |  |
|  | + |  |
|  | + |  |
|  | + |  |

**Check**  Circle the best choice.

## Which of the following is an opinion?

A. *The Wizard of Oz* starts slowly.

B. *The Wizard of Oz* came out in 1939.

C. Dorothy sings "Over the Rainbow."

D. I've seen *The Wizard of Oz* only on TV.

 *Differentiated Activities for Teaching Key Comprehension Skills: Grades 4–6* © 2010 by Martin Lee and Marcia Miller. Scholastic Teaching Resources

# A Family Movie Classic: Activity Sheet

**Read and Understand**  Read the passage. Then answer the questions.

**1.** Why does the reviewer open by describing his or her favorite kinds of movies? _____

_____

**2.** List one fact and one opinion the reviewer includes about *The Wizard of Oz.* _____

_____

_____

**3.** What details support the claim that *The Wizard of Oz* has something for everyone?

_____

**4.** Why does "follow the yellow brick road" have quotation marks? _____

_____

**Word Work: Synonyms and Antonyms**

*Synonyms* are words that have the same or nearly the same meanings. *Antonyms* are words that have opposite meanings. Fill in the table. Give a synonym and an antonym for each word from the passage.

| Word | Synonym | Antonym |
|------|---------|---------|
| hero | champion | villain |
| ending | | |
| recall | | |
| corny | | |
| comforting | | |

**Check**  Circle the best choice.

## Which statement from the review is a fact?

A. It is as exciting to new audiences today as it was back then.

B. The acting, special effects, and dialogue are corny.

C. *The Wizard of Oz* is like a favorite stuffed toy.

D. It actually won for the best music in a movie that year.

# Teaching *Is That You, Jack?*

Students consider the explanations of an unusual occurrence in a science-fiction story.

| Tasks |  Tier 1 <br> Below Level |  Tier 2 <br> On Level |  Tier 3 <br> Above Level |
|---|---|---|---|
| Genre study: science fiction | X | X | X |
| Identify main idea and supporting details | X | X | X |
| Draw conclusions | X | X | X |
| Suggest possible solutions | X | X | X |
| Explore Greek and/or Latin word roots | X | X | X |

## Getting Started

See the tips below for introducing the lesson. Make copies of the reading passage (pages 25–26) and the appropriate leveled activity sheet for each group of learners (pages 27–29).

Access prior knowledge about science fiction and how it compares to both realistic fiction and informational science writing. Build background on recent scientific news about Mars.

---

## Tier 1

- **Main Idea and Details:** Clarify that the narrator claims that his story is true, but the passage is actually fiction. Have students reread the story. Then help them summarize each page. Ask them to highlight the text details they need to answer items 1, 2, and 3.

- **Draw Conclusions:** Remind students to think about clues in the text as well as what they already know. Guide them to answer items 4 and 5. Expect and discuss different responses.

- **Word Work:** Explain that knowing where certain words come from can help us understand other words. Work through this section together. Extend by sharing other Latin roots (see Tiers 2 and 3 for examples from the text).

## Tier 2

- **Draw Conclusions:** Tell students that this comprehension skill is like inferring. For it, we also use given information from the text to make meaning that is not specifically stated. Point out that in this genre, there is a mix of fact and fiction. Allow ample time to share and discuss answers to items 1–4, and have students identify text details that led to their responses.

- **Word Work:** Readers who know common word origins can increase their vocabulary and more readily understand new words. After students complete this section, challenge them to suggest other words with the given origins, such as *dehydrated, monologue,* or *university.*

## Tier 3

- **Draw Conclusions:** You may wish to have students read, discuss, and answer items 1–4 with a partner. Encourage them to combine fact and fiction to make "educated guesses" about the story. After students answer item 3, talk about the significance of knowing that Jack mentioned actual places on Mars. Discuss how this knowledge affects their view of Jack and of the odd event in Chile.

- **Word Work:** Challenge students to discover the origins of these other words in the story: *fantastic, memory, conference, distracted.*

**Skills:**
- Drawing conclusions
- Identifying main idea and details

# Is That You, Jack?
## Reading Passage

This is a true story that I hardly ever tell. People never believe me when I do. They offer all sorts of explanations. They think I'm letting my imagination take over. But I'll tell you if you will keep an open mind.

When I was a kid, a new boy and his folks moved into the last house on our block. The boy's name was Jack. His parents worked at a nearby science research center. Like Jack, they had lots of unruly red hair, and they were tall and thin.

Jack's parents did research at home, too. They tinkered with widgets in their basement. They had more strange tools and instruments than I'd ever seen.

Jack's parents kept to themselves. They never came to our block parties. I rarely spotted them at school or town events. And I hardly ever saw them sitting on their porch just relaxing or chatting with neighbors. My mother explained that some people are more private than others.

The way Jack and his parents spoke gave away the fact that they were not from around here. Their speech didn't sound like most of ours in the neighborhood. They didn't use slang or have a Southern drawl, like the rest of us. In fact, they had no accents at all. I decided they were from somewhere where everyone talks like a TV news host.

Jack and I became quick friends. Jack was honest, modest, and warm-hearted. He also had the widest, brightest smile in the world. It could light up a ballpark at midnight! Our friendship meant a lot to me. We were in the same sixth-grade class in school. Jack rarely spoke up but was a fantastic reader and always scored very well on tests. We did homework together. Jack had the best memory I'd ever seen. Sometimes he retold movie dialogue word for word. Or he spoke to me in Korean or Russian. Jack said he just had a good ear for languages.

Jack was also friends with big Ralphie, Danny, and most of the other kids on the block. When big Ralphie asked Jack where he lived before here, Jack calmly reported that he was from Mars. Yes, *that* Mars.

"Where on Mars?" I asked.

# Is That You, Jack? Reading Passage

"I was born by Hooke Sea," he replied, matter-of-factly.

"Yeah, me too," Ralphie added with a smirk. Everyone laughed.

"We moved to Columbia Hills before coming here," Jack added. What a tease he could be. And he did it all with a poker face. I really admired that.

Jack's family moved away after a few years. Jack said he would go to a private high school in a town I'd never heard of. I felt glum to see him go. We said our good-byes and promised to keep in touch. We both meant it at the time, but it never happened. I guess we were meant to go our separate ways, grow up, and move on with life.

Two years ago, something very odd happened. I still struggle to make sense of it. I'm a scientist myself now. I study the possibility of life elsewhere in the universe. When I was at a conference of astronomers in Chile and was waiting to enter a lecture hall, Jack's parents walked by. At least I think that's who they were; it had been decades since I'd seen them. They looked exactly the same as they had then, tall and skinny with lots of red hair. Was this wishful thinking? Was my imagination going wild again? Was it jet lag?

I approached them. I was ready to introduce myself when I stopped short. A skinny redheaded boy trailed behind them. "Jack, is that you?" I asked in disbelief.

"Yes. My name is Jack," he answered with a smile that lit up the conference hall. "Do I know you, sir?"

That was as much conversation as the tall man with him allowed. "Come on, son," he said crisply. "I've got a lecture to give, and mom's got to start the hydrofoil workshop. Time to go."

Off the three of them went, lost in the crowd in an instant. They never looked back. I stood there, stock-still, for a full minute. What had just happened?

Puzzled, I gathered myself and entered the lecture hall. It was packed with people like me, eager to learn about the recent discovery of water on Mars. The speakers gave their presentations, which were probably fascinating. They debated whether water means that Mars could support life. But I was totally distracted and heard little of it all. I was thinking about Jack.

I'm still bewildered as I share this tale. But what I'm telling you really happened. I'll always wonder what—or who—I saw that day.

# ◆ Is That You, Jack? Activity Sheet

**Read and Understand** ) Read the passage. Then answer the questions.

**1.** How did the narrator come to know Jack? _____

_____

**2.** List two ways that Jack's family was different from the others. _____

_____

**3.** What did the narrator like about Jack? Write three adjectives he uses to describe Jack.

_____

**4.** What was odd about Jack so many years later? _____

**5.** Who do you think Jack was? _____

_____

**Word Work: Word Origins** )

*Imagination* comes from the Latin root *imago*. *Imago* means *picture* or *idea*. *Imago* is also the root of other words. Use the meaning of *imago* to explain each word below.

*image* _____

*imagine* _____

*imagination* _____

**Check** ) Circle the best choice.

**Why does the narrator want readers to "keep an open mind"?**

A. He knows that the story will be hard to believe.

B. He can't remember the most important details.

C. He feels embarrassed about sharing this story.

D. He wants readers to choose their friends carefully.

# Is That You, Jack? Activity Sheet

**Read and Understand** Read the passage. Then answer the questions.

**1.** Why would the narrator ask readers to keep an open mind? _____

_____

**2.** Why did Jack's parents have so many tools and instruments? _____

_____

**3.** What was the narrator doing in Chile? _____

**4.** What was odd about seeing Jack and his parents in Chile? _____

_____

**Word Work: Word Origins**

Many English words came from Greek (G) or Latin (L) roots. Read each root and its meaning. Then write a word from the story that has the root and matches the definition.

| Greek or Latin Root/Meaning | | English Word | Definition |
|---|---|---|---|
| *astron* (G) | star | | scientists who study the stars |
| *hydor* (G) | water | | special kind of fast boat |
| *legere* (L) | to read | | to read to a group |
| *logos* (G) | speech | | speech between two or more people |

**Check** Circle the best choice.

## Which is the least likely reason the boys lost touch after Jack moved away?

A. They never really liked each other that much.

B. Jack and his family didn't visit again.

C. Each boy became involved with new friends and activities.

D. Jack's parents prevented him from keeping in touch.

Name _____     Date _____

 # Is That You, Jack? Activity Sheet

**Read and Understand**  Read the passage. Then answer the questions.

**1.** Why might Jack's parents have kept to themselves? _____

_____

**2.** Hooke Sea and Columbia Hills are real places on Mars. Why would Jack mention them?

_____

**3.** How do you know that years passed in this story? _____

_____

**4.** What might explain what the narrator saw in Chile? _____

_____

**Word Work: Word Origins**

Many English words have Greek (G) or Latin (L) roots. Read each root and its meaning.
Then write an English word from the story that has the root and give its definition.

| Greek or Latin Root/Meaning | | English Word | Definition |
|---|---|---|---|
| *astron* (G) | star | | |
| *hydor* (G) | water | | |
| *legere* (L) | to read | | |
| *logos* (G) | speech | | |
| *universus* (L) | turned into one | | |

**Check**  Circle the best choice.

**Which is the least likely reason the boys lost touch after Jack moved away?**

A. They never really liked each other that much.

B. Jack and his family didn't visit again.

C. Each boy became involved with new friends and activities.

D. Jack's parents prevented him from keeping in touch.

# Teaching **Shades of Meaning**

Students read an informational article about the history and uses of sunglasses.

| Tasks | ◆ Tier 1 Below Level | ● Tier 2 On Level | ⬠ Tier 3 Above Level |
|---|---|---|---|
| Identify main idea and supporting details | X | X | X |
| Recognize cause-and-effect relationships | X | | X |
| Use chronological order to comprehend | X | X | X |
| Make inferences | | X | X |
| Use the suffix -ly | X | X | X |

## Getting Started

See the tips below for introducing the lesson. Make copies of the reading passage (pages 31) and the appropriate leveled activity sheet for each group of learners (pages 32–34).

Access prior knowledge about sunglasses and their use. Build background on the history of vision-correcting lenses and the different names for sunglasses

 ## Tier 1

- **Chronological Order:** Discuss the organizational style of the passage. Guide students to see that the author tells the history of sunglasses in time order, beginning with their first use in ancient China.

- **Main Idea and Details:** Review topic sentences. Have students identify the topic sentence or main idea of each paragraph. Help them find supporting details for items 1–4.

- **Cause and Effect** For item 5, invite students to brainstorm current examples of the advertising practice of using celebrities to sell products.

- **Word Work:** If appropriate, introduce spelling rules for adding -ly when base words end in le or y.

 ## Tier 2

- **Make Inferences:** For item 1, discuss that the title only hints at what the article is about. For item 3, invite students to brainstorm reasons for the name *coolers*.

- **Chronological Order:** For item 2, review the first bulleted tip for below-level learners.

- **Main Idea and Details:** For item 4, clarify that although the topic sentence of Paragraph 4 is its first sentence, a topic sentence can appear anywhere in a paragraph.

- **Word Work:** Have students list four more words with the -*ly* suffix that are formed from words ending in *le* or *y*.

 ## Tier 3

- **Make Inferences:** For item 1, discuss that the title is a play on words and only hints at what the article is about.

- **Main Idea and Details:** For item 3, explain that a topic sentence can appear anywhere in a paragraph, but is frequently the first, second, or final sentence.

- **Cause and Effect:** Discuss items 2 and 4, focusing on the cause-and-effect relationships.

- **Chronological Order:** After students answer item 5, challenge them to suggest ways other than chronologically to organize an informational article.

- **Word Work:** Challenge students to use each -*ly* word in a meaningful sentence.

# Shades of Meaning

There are many names for sunglasses. You might call them *shades* or *dark glasses*. People in India call them *glares* or *coolers*. Australians know them as *sunnies*. Sunglasses by any name all do the same useful job: they protect our eyes from the harmful glare of the sun. Sunglasses have been around for nearly a thousand years.

The first sunglasses were invented in China, although no one knows exactly when. Those dark lenses did not block the sun. They had quite a different purpose. They were worn to let judges hide their faces in court. Judges did not want to give away any clues as to what they were thinking. It's hard to tell what someone is feeling or thinking when you cannot see his or her eyes.

Italians brought vision-correcting glasses to China in about 1430. Those lenses were dark. And guess what? Most were still used by judges. So dark glasses were worn mainly indoors, where there was no sun to block!

It is only recently that sunglasses have become commonly worn. The turning point came in 1929. In that year, Sam Foster introduced his sunglasses. He sold his cheap shades at a store on the Boardwalk of Atlantic City, New Jersey. They became very popular right away. Foster named his company *Foster Grant*. Movie stars wore Sam Foster's glasses. That's how they got the nickname "sunglasses of the stars." Celebrities wore them in newspaper and magazine ads. These ads asked, "Who's that behind the Foster Grants?" Sunglasses became all the rage. Everyone wanted a pair!

Today's shades come in all styles, shapes, colors, and sizes. People wear sunglasses for many reasons. Soldiers and pilots use them to cut the sun's glare. Astronauts in space wear special sunglasses to protect their eyes from radiation. Athletes use them, too. Swimmers, skiers, cyclists, and mountain climbers wear special kinds of shades as they compete in their sports.

Some people wear sunglasses to hide their eyes. Others wear them to hide their identity. But many people simply like how sunglasses make them look. Some people wear sunglasses day and night, indoors and out. Fashion designers have taken notice. Many now have their own brands of sunglasses. Styles change all the time, and millions of buyers want to stay up to date. So who's behind the coolest shades you've ever seen?

# ◆ Shades of Meaning: Activity Sheet

( **Read and Understand** )  Read the passage. Then answer the questions.

**1.** Sunglasses were first used in _____.

**2.** Four other names for sunglasses are _____

_____.

**3.** Sunglasses became common after Sam Foster began selling them in the year _____.

**4.** Name four sports in which athletes wear sunglasses, according to the passage.

_____

**5.** Foster's sunglasses got the nickname "Sunglasses of the Stars" because _____

_____.

( **Word Work: Suffix** *-ly* )

*Suffixes* are groups of letters added to the end of a word. They change the meanings of words or make new words. The suffix *-ly* means "how" or "in a certain way."

Quick<u>ly</u> means "in a quick way" and dark<u>ly</u> means "in a dark way."
Read each word below. Use the base word to help you figure out and write the meaning.

| Word With *-ly* | Meaning |
|---|---|
| silently | |
| recently | |
| seriously | |
| sadly | |

( **Check** )  Circle the best choice.

## Which is the topic sentence of Paragraph 4 in the article?

A. The turning point came in 1929.

B. Foster named his company *Foster Grant*.

C. They became popular right away.

D. It is only recently that sunglasses have become commonly worn.

Name _____     Date _____

#  Shades of Meaning: Activity Sheet

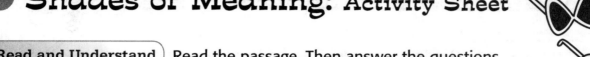

( **Read and Understand** )  Read the passage. Then answer the questions.

**1.** Read the first paragraph. What do you expect to learn by reading the rest of the passage? _____

**2.** Where and when were sunglasses first used? _____

**3.** In which country are sunglasses known as *coolers*? _____

**4.** What is the topic sentence for Paragraph 4? _____

_____

**5.** How does the author organize the data about the history of sunglasses? _____

_____

( **Word Work: Suffix** *-ly* )

*Suffixes* are groups of letters added to the end of a word that change its meaning. The suffix *-ly* means "how" or "in a certain way."

Quick<u>ly</u> means "in a quick way."        Easi<u>ly</u> means "in an easy way."

Add -**ly** to each underlined word. Write the new word to the right.

| in a <u>silent</u> way | |
|---|---|
| at a <u>recent</u> time | |
| in a <u>humble</u> voice | |
| in a <u>happy</u> manner | |

( **Check** )  Circle the best choice.

## Which is the topic sentence of Paragraph 5 in the article?

A. Soldiers and pilots use them to cut the sun's glare.

B. Today's shades come in all styles, shapes, colors, and sizes.

C. People wear sunglasses for many reasons.

D. Athletes use them, too.

Name _____   Date _____

# ⬠ Shades of Meaning: Activity Sheet

**Read and Understand**   Read the passage. Then answer the questions.

**1.** Read the first paragraph. What do you expect to learn by reading the rest of the article? _____

**2.** Why did judges in China wear sunglasses? _____

**3.** What is the topic sentence for Paragraph 5? _____

_____

**4.** Why do you think fashion designers are adding sunglasses to their lines of clothing?

_____

**5.** How would does the author organize the data about the history of sunglasses?

_____

**Word Work: Suffix -ly**

Adding a *suffix* to the end of a word changes the word's meaning or makes a new word. The suffix -ly means "how" or "in a certain way."

Quick<u>ly</u> means "in a quick way."          Easi<u>ly</u> means "in an easy way."

Add **-ly** to each underlined word. Write the new word in a sentence to the right.

| | |
|---|---|
| in a <u>silent</u> way | |
| at a <u>recent</u> time | |
| in a <u>humble</u> voice | |
| in a <u>happy</u> manner | |

**Check**   Circle the best choice.

## Which is not given as a reason why sunglasses became so popular in 1929?

A. They were inexpensive to buy.          C. Movie stars were wearing them.

B. They improved peoples' lives.          D. They were advertised and marketed cleverly.

# Teaching **Two Rice Cakes**

Students analyze a Vietnamese folktale about a contest to become the next king.

## Skills:
- Comparing and contrasting
- Determining causes and effects
- Identifying conflict in a story

| Tasks | ◆ Tier 1 Below Level | ● Tier 2 On Level | ⬠ Tier 3 Above Level |
|---|:---:|:---:|:---:|
| Read and interpret folktales | X | X | X |
| Identify conflict in a story | X | X | X |
| Determine cause and effect |  | X | X |
| Compare and contrast story elements | X | X |  |
| Identify symbolism |  | X | X |
| Identify and differentiate homophones | X | X | X |

## Getting Started

See the tips below for introducing the lesson. Make copies of the reading passage (page 36) and the appropriate leveled activity sheet for each group of learners (pages 37–39).

Access prior knowledge of folktales and commonalities between them. Build background on Vietnam and its culture

---

## ◆ Tier 1

- **Conflict:** Point out that good stories have a character with a problem or a conflict to resolve. Identify main conflicts in stories students know. Discuss why it would be hard for this king simply to choose a prince to follow him. Then have students answer item 1 in their own words.

- **Compare and Contrast:** Remind students to *compare* like features and to *contrast* unlike features. Help them answer item 2.

- **Cause and Effect:** Use If/Then statements to focus students on cause and effect: *IF (action takes place) . . . THEN (effect happens).* Have them use this device to answer items 3 and 4.

- **Word Work:** Since homophones commonly cause comprehension and spelling problems, it's best for students to learn to recognize them. Work through this section together.

##  Tier 2

- **Conflict:** Explain that a problem or conflict builds interest and moves a story along. Ask students why the king didn't simply pick one of his sons to follow him as king. Then have them answer item 1.

- **Compare and Contrast:** Have students identify text details that show how Tiet-Lieu differs from his brothers. Then have them answer item 2.

- **Cause and Effect:** Suggest that students remember the central conflict and put themselves in the king's place to better answer item 3.

- **Symbolism:** Define *symbolism* as using one thing to represent another. Have students reread the opening sentence of the folktale to help them answer item 4.

- **Word Work:** See the fourth bulleted tip for Tier 1. Have students complete the table independently.

##  Tier 3

- **Conflict:** Discuss the problems any leader would have in choosing a successor. Then have students answer item 1.

- **Cause and Effect:** Before students answer item 2, talk about what the tale suggests about Tiet-Lieu's brothers, and what it omits.

- **Symbolism:** Review *symbolism* as letting one thing stand for another. As needed, guide students to review the opening sentence of the tale to help them answer item 3.

- **Word Work:** See the previous Word Work tips. Challenge students to list other homophones.

# Two Rice Cakes:
## Reading Passage

*A FOLKTALE FROM VIETNAM*

When Hung-Vuong was king, the people believed that the sky was round and the earth was square. Hung-Vuong had twenty-two sons. One day he called them all before him. He said, "I am old. I need an heir. So there will be a contest. Each of you shall travel our land. You shall find a food special enough to please me. The prince whose dish is best shall become king. You have until spring."

Hung-Vuong secretly hoped that the quest would teach the princes about the land one of them would rule, but he said nothing as his sons bowed to him. Then the princes left to seek the perfect food—that is, all except the youngest son. He went home to his wife and children. Tiet-Lieu was unlike his brothers. He was not a poet, a hunter, or a warrior. He was just a farmer.

Some princes hunted for animals and birds. The dishes that followed were fit for a king. Others sailed the waters for fish or seafood. They tried grand dishes, too. But Tiet-Lieu merely tended his farm. When his rice was ripe, he plucked some golden grains from a long stalk. Their delicate scent gave him an idea.

He and his family harvested the rice. Then Tiet-Lieu ground it into flour. His wife added water to form a soft paste for rice cakes. Next, he built a fire as his children wrapped rice cakes in banana leaves. They baked two large trays of them.

When the rice cakes were done, Tiet-Lieu unwrapped one from each tray to taste. To his surprise, one was square and the other round. The family unwrapped the rest. All rice cakes were either round or square. Tiet-Lieu liked what he saw.

In spring, all the princes returned to offer the king their special foods. One prince made fish with wild mushrooms. Another presented roasted peacock on flower petals. A third offered prawns in ginger. These and all other dishes were cooked and served with great care.

Then Tiet-Lieu came forward. He served the king one square rice cake and one round one. The other princes sneered at such a modest offering, but the king tasted this dish, as he did with the others.

At last, the king decided. "The highest honor goes to Tiet-Lieu," he said. "His food was the purest of all because he used only the rice he grew himself, and water from our own land. His helpers were his own family. Tiet-Lieu understands our people."

The emperor and twenty-one princes bowed to Tiet-Lieu, the new king.

Name _____  Date _____

 # Two Rice Cakes: Activity Sheet

**Read and Understand** ) Read the passage. Then answer the questions.

**1.** What problem did the king have? _____

_____

**2.** In what ways was Tiet-Lieu unlike his brothers? _____

_____

**3.** Why did the other princes look down on Tiet-Lieu's rice cakes? _____

_____

**4.** What impressed the king so much about the rice cakes? _____

_____

**Word Work: Homophones**

*Homophones* are words that sound alike but have different spellings and meanings.
Read the sentences below. Circle the two homophones in each sentence.

- The new heir took a deep breath of fresh air.

- The young prince prints his name.

- We sent for lotion with a lemon scent.

- That brand of flour has a red flower on the label.

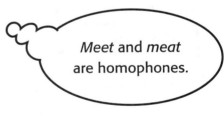

*Meet* and *meat*
are homophones.

**Check** ) Circle the best choice.

**What was the king's solution to the problem in this tale?**

A. He decided to grow rice.

B. He needed to decide who should be the next king.

C. He tried to fish for food.

D. He compared the dish that each prince brought him.

#  Two Rice Cakes: Activity Sheet

**Read and Understand**  Read the passage. Then answer the questions.

**1.** What was the king secretly seeking in setting up the contest? _____

_____

**2.** In what ways was Tiet-Lieu unlike his brothers? _____

_____

**3.** What pleased the king so much about Tiet-Lieu's offering? _____

_____

**4.** What is special about the shapes of the rice cakes Tiet-Lieu made? _____

_____

**Word Work: Homophones**

*Homophones* are words that sound alike but have different spellings and meanings, like *meet* and *meat*. In the first column write a homophone from the story that matches the given meaning. Then write your own homophone in the last column.

| Homophone in Tale | Meaning | Homophone |
|---|---|---|
| heir | next in line to rule | air |
| | son of a king | |
| | fragrance, odor | |
| | colorful part of a plant | |

**Check**  Circle the best choice.

**Why did the other princes sneer at Tiet-Lieu's rice cakes?**

A. The other princes wished they had made rice cakes.

B. Rice cakes seemed to be too plain an offering.

C. The other princes disliked their youngest brother.

D. They thought Tiet-Lieu was disrespecting the king.

# Two Rice Cakes: Activity Sheet

**Read and Understand** ) Read the passage. Then answer the questions.

**1.** What was the king secretly seeking in setting up the contest? _____

_____

**2.** Why did the other princes look down on Tiet-Lieu's rice cakes? _____

_____

**3.** What is special about the shapes of the rice cakes? _____

_____

**4.** What important values does this tale teach? Explain. _____

_____

**Word Work: Homophones**

*Homophones* are words that sound alike but have different spellings and meanings, like *meet* and *meat*. For each homophone listed, find a homophone from the folktale. Write the homophone and its meaning in the table.

| Homophone | Homophone in Tale | Meaning |
|-----------|-------------------|---------|
| air | heir | next in line to rule |
| prints | | |
| flower | | |
| tern | | |
| cent, sent | | |

**Check** ) Circle the best choice.

**How do Tiet-Lieu's rice cakes best represent Vietnam?**

A. Rice is an important part of the Vietnamese diet.

B. They reflect knowledge and respect of its people and ways.

C. It takes a whole family to prepare good rice cakes.

D. They were round like the sky and square like the earth.

# Teaching
## School Schedule Debate

Students read the speeches of two debaters about lengthening the time students spend in school.

| Tasks | ◆ Tier 1 Below Level | ● Tier 2 On Level | ⬠ Tier 3 Above Level |
|---|---|---|---|
| Identify main ideas and supporting details | X | X | X |
| Distinguish facts from opinions | X | X | X |
| Compare and contrast points of view | | X | X |
| Use antonyms | X | X | X |

## Getting Started

See the tips below for introducing the lesson. Make copies of the reading passage (pages 41–42) and the appropriate leveled activity sheet for each group of learners (pages 43–45).

Access prior knowledge by discussing what students know about the length of the school day in different schools around the country and the world, today and long ago. Build background on the features and styles of a formal debate.

---

 ## Tier 1

- **Main Idea and Details:** Point out that this selection has two major parts: (1) Karen's views and (2) Hassan's views. As students prepare to answer each item, have them highlight details in the text that support their thinking. Point out that *teachers*, *parents*, and *students* are italicized in Karen's speech to focus readers on what each group thinks. Help students locate the words in the paragraph about parents that best help them answer item 3 (*most of all*).

- **Fact and Opinion:** Clarify the difference between a fact and an opinion by discussing realistic examples students will recognize. Have students cite cue words they use to identify the differences.

- **Word Work:** You may wish to have students work in pairs to complete the table.

 ## Tier 2

- **Main Idea and Details:** For all items, have students identify specific text details that support their answers. Ask students to explain why *teachers*, *parents*, and *students* are italicized in parts of Karen's speech.

- **Compare and Contrast:** For items 2 and 5, guide students to recognize that although debaters may present contrasting views on a topic, they may also agree on certain points.

- **Fact and Opinion:** Discuss the role of an opinion in a debate. Point out that to be valid, it should be supported by facts. For the Check item, ask students why answer choices A, C, and D are opinions.

 ## Tier 3

- **Main Idea and Details:** Explain that all debaters present ideas and supporting details. However, effective debaters also consider tactics, organization, and convincing language.

- **Compare and Contrast:** Clarify that although debaters present contrasting views on a topic, they may agree on some points. For item 4, let small groups debate who made the stronger case and why.

- **Distinguish Fact From Opinion:** Have students volunteer to offer statements that are either a fact or an opinion, and then let the class determine which each one is. Discuss how facts and opinions are intertwined in debates.

**Skills:**
- Recognizing main ideas and supporting details
- Distinguishing fact from opinion
- Comparing/contrasting points of view

# School Schedule Debate:
## Reading Passage

*Two students at Webster School are holding a debate. Karen and Hassan are debating whether the length of the school day and school year are fine as they are, or whether they should be longer. After each student makes his or her case, there will be time for questions. Karen goes first, based on a coin toss.*

## Karen's Argument

Hi. I am Karen Lindsey. I have been a student in this school for six years. I like it here very much. I think we have a good school.

But my reading tells me that many schools across the country are in trouble. I read that American students are falling behind the kids in many other countries. I read that our test scores are lower than theirs are. I read that many kids who go to college first need to take basic reading and math courses before they can take college-level classes. I also read that our schools are not turning out enough mathematicians, engineers, doctors, and scientists. American students know very little about our history and the history of other places. I think this is very sad. I think it is urgent that we fix this problem.

So I very strongly believe that we need to lengthen each school day. And I believe just as strongly that the school year should be longer, too. Doing both is a good start. It shows that we are working to try to make the situation better in all schools.

I think *teachers* will agree with me. The way things are now, teachers can barely get through teaching what they are supposed to. Since they need to spend lots of time preparing us for tests and because we have so many holidays, they don't have enough time to cover all the topics they are supposed to. They simply need more time with students, especially students who need extra help. Plus, I'm sure teachers would be glad for the additional pay they would get.

I think that *parents* will agree with me. Having a longer school day and a longer school year means less money spent on childcare and babysitting. It means spending less money on summer vacation activities for kids, too. It also means more time for clubs, projects, and other school activities. It means more time for subjects that don't get enough attention now. But most of all, parents will appreciate that we will learn more if we are in school longer.

And I think *students* will agree with me, too. A longer school day means more time for the core subjects. It also means more time for subjects students like—computer lab, art, music, or drama classes. It can mean less homework. And less homework leaves more time for fun stuff. If students think about it seriously, they'll understand that it's better in the long run to spend more time in school now.

Having longer school days and school years makes so much sense. We've got the buildings, we've got the fields, we've got the teachers and we've got the staffs. All we need now is to get on board. Extra time in school is time well spent. And everyone will reap the benefits. Thank you very much.

## Hassan's Argument

Hello, fellow students. I am Hassan Walid. Like Karen, I like it here at Webster School very much. But unlike Karen, I think that increasing school time is a bad idea. It's an idea that misses the point by a mile.

You see, I know that a mile is 1,760 yards long and 5,280 feet long. I know that a mile is equal to 1.6093 kilometers and to 1,609.3 meters. Why do I know these things? I know them because I pay attention, work hard in class, and do the best job I can on my homework. We don't need longer school days or years. We need to put the time we already have to better use. The *hours* don't need to change. *We* need to change. If we are not competing well with kids in other countries, it's because our teachers are not putting in enough effort, and neither are students. We need to try harder. And we can do it.

Karen says that teachers can't cover the curriculum in the time they have. I say, help teachers do their job better. Get better textbooks, for example. She says that test-prep takes away needed hours. I say, have fewer tests, but have better ones. She says that some students need more individual attention. I say, don't add on more *hours*, add on more *teachers* and more *classrooms* and more *peer tutors*.

Teachers don't want longer school days or school years any more than we kids do. Why would they? They work hard enough. And to pay teachers for extra work makes no *sense*—it just costs more *cents*, lots of them. You would have to pay much more for the salaries of not only teachers, but also school staff. You would have to pay for larger electric and gas bills as well for all school services, too. If we're spending money, let's spend it on better books and equipment.

Kids certainly don't want more hours in the classroom. They want more interesting hours there. And I think we'll all agree that the school day is plenty long enough right now—maybe even too long. My older brother is in the tenth grade. He's on the track team and doesn't even get home until 6:15 or so. He doesn't even get started on his homework until 8:00! Isn't that a long enough day? And some want even longer days? Not me. Thank you for listening.

# School Schedule Debate: Activity Sheet

**Read and Understand**  Read the passage. Then answer the questions.

**1.** Which student says the school day and school year should stay the same? _____

**2.** Why does Karen argue that teachers would want longer school days and years?

_____

_____

**3.** What does Karen say is the *main* reason parents would agree with her? _____

_____

_____

**4.** What example does Hassan use to argue that the school day is long enough as it is?

_____

**Word Work: Antonyms**

*Antonyms* are words that have the opposite or nearly opposite meaning.

Find each word listed in the left column in the debate and see how it is used. Then write an antonym for it in the column at the right.

| Word From Debate | Antonym |
|---|---|
| many | |
| basic | |
| lengthen | |
| agree | |
| better | |

**Check**  Circle the best choice.

**Debaters mix facts and opinion. Which of the following statements is a *fact*?**

A. "It's an idea that misses the point by a mile."

B. "A mile is equal to 1.6093 kilometers."

C. "I'm sure teachers would be glad for the additional pay."

D. "Having longer school days makes so much sense."

# School Schedule Debate: Activity Sheet

**Read and Understand** Read the passage. Then answer the questions.

**1.** Which debater argues that our educational woes could be fixed *without* lengthening the school day or year? _____

**2.** Who believes that American students have fallen behind? _____

**3.** What reasons does Karen give for why students will agree with her? _____

_____

**4.** According to Hassan, what can schools do so that teachers have enough time to cover their subjects fully? _____

_____

**5.** On what points do the two debaters agree? _____

_____

**Word Work: Antonyms**

*Antonyms* are words that have the opposite or nearly opposite meaning.

Complete the table.

| Word From Passage | Antonym |
|---|---|
| longer | |
| barely | |
| | advanced |
| individual | |

**Check** Circle the best choice.

**Which of the following is a statement of *fact*?**

A. "And everyone will reap the benefits."

B. "I have been a student in this school for six years."

C. "I'm sure teachers would be glad for the additional pay."

D. "Kids certainly don't want more hours in the classroom."

# School Schedule Debate: Activity Sheet

**Read and Understand** ) Read the passage. Then answer the questions.

**1.** According to Hassan, what must change in order for students to get a better

education? _____

_____

**2.** According to Karen, what reasons do *both* parents and kids agree on in support of

lengthening time in school? _____

_____

**3.** On what points do the two debaters agree? _____

**4.** In your opinion, which debater makes a stronger case? Explain. _____

_____

**Word Work: Antonyms** )

*Antonyms* are words that have the opposite or nearly the opposite meaning.

Complete the table.

| Word From Passage | Antonym |
|---|---|
| longer | |
| barely | |
| | advanced |
| individual | |
| | unessential |

**Check** ) Circle the best choice.

**Which of the following is a statement of *fact*?**

A. "And everyone will reap the benefits."

B. "I have been a student in this school for six years."

C. "I'm sure teachers would be glad for the additional pay."

D. "Having longer school days makes so much sense."

# Teaching
## The Navajo Code Talkers

**Skills:**
- Recognizing author's purpose
- Identifying cause-and-effect relationships
- Drawing conclusions

Students read an informational article about a group of American patriots during World War II.

| Tasks | Tier 1 Below Level | Tier 2 On Level | Tier 3 Above Level |
|---|---|---|---|
| Recognize the author's purpose | X | X | X |
| Identify cause-and-effect relationships | X | X | X |
| Compare and contrast | | X | X |
| Draw conclusions | X | X | X |
| Use the prefixes *un-* and *dis-* | X | X | |
| Use thematic words: military terms | | | X |

## Getting Started

See the tips below for introducing the lesson. Make copies of the reading passage (pages 47–48) and the appropriate leveled activity sheet for each group of learners (pages 49–51).

Access prior knowledge about World War II, especially battles in the Pacific against the Japanese. Build background on the basics of the war in terms of the time frame and countries involved. Then also talk about the Navajo people.

 **Tier 1**

- **Cause and Effect:** Guide students to reread the first four paragraphs and highlight supporting details before they begin item 1. For item 2, discuss the cause-and-effect relationship between Johnston's experiences and his solution.

- **Draw Conclusions:** Ask students to share their responses to item 3. Talk about why Native American languages were useful in making military codes.

- **Author's Purpose:** For item 4, point out that the achievements of the Code Talkers still remain mostly unknown and unappreciated, so this may be a clue to the author's purpose.

- **Word Work:** Follow up by guiding students to use each word with a prefix in a meaningful sentence.

 **Tier 2**

- **Author's Purpose:** For item 1, point out that the wartime contributions of the Code Talkers are largely unknown to most people to this day, and this may be a clue to the author's purpose.

- **Cause and Effect:** Direct students to the key sentences in Paragraphs 2, 3, and 4 for item 2.

- **Compare and Contrast:** For item 3, have students contrast the success of the Navajo language code with the failures of the codes it replaced.

- **Draw Conclusions:** Have students share text details for item 4.

- **Word Work:** Follow up by having students write a another sentence about the article for each word.

 **Tier 3**

- **Author's Purpose:** Have students look for clues in the text to suggest the author's purpose. Ask students to give examples of other purposes an author may have in writing nonfiction.

- **Cause and Effect:** To answer item 2, students should consider the circumstances before and after the army began to use the Navajo Code Talkers. Have them discuss results of the change in plan.

- **Draw Conclusions:** For item 3, point out that written languages are more easily understood and translated than unwritten ones. Have students support their responses to item 4 with text details.

- **Word Work:** Ask students to identify other military terms in the article and to suggest any other examples they may know from reading or watching programs about the military.

Name _____  Date _____

**Skills:**
- Recognizing author's purpose
- Identifying cause-and-effect relationships
- Drawing conclusions

# The Navajo Code Talkers

The words *chay-da-gahi*, *gini*, and *ne-eh-mah* come from the Navajo language. But they have more in common than that. Each word was a term used in a very special secret code. It was a code that befuddled the Japanese forces during World War II. In code, *chay-da-gahi* (turtle) meant *tank*. *Gini* (chicken hawk) meant *dive-bomber*. And *ne-eh-mah* (our mother) meant *America*. The code was never cracked. It was the only unbreakable code ever used in modern wars. Many American lives were saved because the opposing Japanese military could never figure it out.

Armies at war use codes to keep their plans secret. Enemies try to figure out their opponents' codes in order to learn their strategies. Early in World War II, the Japanese intelligence experts were able to break the American codes. This was very troubling because it let the Japanese know in advance what our soldiers were going to do. It also allowed them to learn where and when they were going to do it.

Japanese soldiers used what they learned to fool the Americans. They used fake commands to disrupt plans and plan ambushes. Their forces kept one step ahead of ours. American leaders knew that they had a big problem. They needed a better way to send and receive messages. They needed a code too tricky for the Japanese code-breakers to crack.

A man named Phillip Johnston came to the rescue. He grew up with the Navajo in Arizona because his father worked there. He knew about the code problem and thought of a solution. Johnston had fought in World War I. In that war, the American Army successfully used other Native American languages to make

Navajo Code Talkers, Marine Corps, Bougainville (New Guinea) December, 1943

© Defense Department, Marine Corps

codes. Johnston spoke Navajo. He was one of very few outsiders who did. He knew that the language was very hard to learn. He also knew that it had no alphabet. Johnston believed that a code using the Navajo language could be very successful.

# The Navajo Code Talkers

**(continued)**

Johnston met with top military leaders. He presented his idea. Then he modeled how the code might work. The generals were very impressed. They asked him to start a program with Navajo speakers. The Navajo soldiers worked as Marine Corps Radio Operators. But they were known as the Code Talkers.

Johnston began with twenty-nine Code Talkers in early 1942. There were more than 400 by the end of the war. All were young Navajo men, some as young as fifteen. Most had never been away from their villages. Johnston and his Navajo recruits created their code at Camp Pendleton in California. They practiced until they were very good at it.

The Navajo language code began with about 200 terms. It was very quick to use. Coded messages used to take a half hour to send using the machines of the time. Now they could be sent in 20 seconds!

After their training, the Navajo Code Talkers went to the Pacific to work with the Marines. The generals quickly appreciated the special skills these men from the Arizona desert brought. They were amazed that they never wrote down any part of the code. The Code Talkers knew it all by heart.

*Code Talkers sent and received more than 800 radio messages to help the U.S. Marines win the key battle of Iwo Jima in 1945.*

© Joe Rosenthal/Associated Press

The Navajo code grew to more than 600 terms by 1945, when World War II ended. It was so successful that the Marines used it again in the Korean War in the early 1950s. The code remained secret for almost twenty more years. And the Navajo Code Talkers remained unknown heroes. In 2001, these brave Native American war heroes finally received Congressional Medals of Honor.

Today, there are still few people who know the story of the Navajo Code Talkers. Back in Arizona, the Code Talkers were humble farmers and sheep herders, but in World War II, they were courageous soldiers. They played a role in saving many lives. Their efforts helped to speed along the end of the war. Our country is in their debt.

Only a few of the Code Talkers are alive today. They are now in their 80s and 90s. Not all of their stories have been told. One way to learn more about these heroes is to contact The *Navajo Code Talker Association*. This group is working to preserve their unique history.

To learn more about the Navajo Code Talkers, you can visit their Website: **www.navajocodetalkers.org**.

 *Differentiated Activities for Teaching Key Comprehension Skills: Grades 4–6* © 2010 by Martin Lee and Marcia Miller. Scholastic Teaching Resources

Name _____  Date _____

 # The Navajo Code Talkers: Activity Sheet

**Read and Understand**  Read the passage. Then answer the questions.

**1.** Why did the American forces in World War II need a new secret code? _____

_____

**2.** What was Phillip Johnston's plan for solving the army's code problem? _____

_____

**3.** Why was the Navajo code successful?_____

_____

**4.** What was the author's purpose in writing this article? _____

_____

**Word Work: Prefixes *un-* and *dis-***

*Prefixes* are word parts added to the beginning of a word. The prefix *un-* means "not," as in <u>un</u>breakable. The prefix *dis-* means "not" or "opposite of," as in <u>dis</u>agree.

Circle the prefix in each word at the left. Draw a line to match each word with its meaning.

| Word With Prefix | Meaning |
|---|---|
| unknown | not common |
| dishonest | not known |
| disloyal | not honest |
| uncommon | not loyal |

**Check**  Circle the best choice.

## Which best describes the author's view of the Code Talkers?

A. The author thinks they were great military leaders.

B. The author greatly values their skills and military contributions.

C. The author loves their unique language.

D. The author thinks they were good farmers and sheep herders.

# ● The Navajo Code Talkers: Activity Sheet

**Read and Understand**  Read the passage. Then answer the questions.

**1.** What was the author's purpose was in writing this piece? _____

_____

**2.** What problem did the American military face early in the war against the Japanese,

and how did they solve it? _____

_____

**3.** What was the effect of using the Navajo code? _____

_____

**4.** Why does the author believe that we owe much to the Code Talkers? _____

_____

**Word Work: Prefixes *un-* and *dis-***

*The prefix un- and dis- mean "not," as in <u>un</u>breakable and <u>dis</u>continue.*

*Prefixes* are word parts added to the beginning of a word that change its meaning. Complete each sentence with a word below.

**disrupt**    **unknown**    **disqualify**    **unfamiliar**

Most people are _____ with the Navajo language.

Breaking an enemy's codes can _____ its military plans.

What could _____ someone from being a code breaker?

The contributions of the Navajo Code Talkers are _____ to many.

**Check**  Circle the best choice.

## Which best describes the author's view of the Code Talkers?

A. The author thinks good farmers made good code makers.

B. The author very much values their courage, skills, and contributions.

C. The author loves their unique language.

D. The author thinks they learned the code quickly.

Name _____   Date _____

 # The Navajo Code Talkers: Activity Sheet

**Read and Understand** | Read the passage. Then answer the questions.

**1.** What was the author's purpose in writing this article? _____

_____

**2.** What strategy did the American army come up with to confuse Japanese intelligence

experts? _____

_____

**3.** Why might the Americans have used Native American languages as military codes?

_____

**4.** What conclusion can you draw about the value of secrecy and codes in wartime?

_____

_____

**Word Work: Military Terms**

There are military words used in this passage. Complete each sentence with a word below.

**ambush    command    force    recruit**

Phillip Johnston's plan was to _____ Navajo men as code breakers.

The general gave the _____ to move troops forward.

An estimated _____ of twenty marines entered the town.

Breaking a code, meant one side could _____ enemy soldiers at will.

**Check** | Circle the best choice.

**Which was not a reason for using the Navajo language to create a successful code?**

A  It was spoken by very few people.          C  It had very many short words.

B  It was an unwritten language.               D  It was hard to learn.

# Teaching
# Eye-Witness to History

**Skills:**
- Understanding the element of setting
- Identifying author's purpose
- Identifying main idea and supporting details

Students read about the Wright Brothers' pioneering work through historical fiction.

| Tasks | ◆ Tier 1 Below Level | ● Tier 2 On Level | ⬠ Tier 3 Above Level |
|---|:---:|:---:|:---:|
| Understand setting as a narrative element | X | X | X |
| Identify author's purpose in historical fiction | X | X | X |
| Identify main idea and supporting details | X | X | X |
| Sequence events in a story | | X | X |
| Use vivid verbs | X | X | X |

## Getting Started

See the tips below for introducing the lesson. Make copies of the reading passage (pages 53–54) and the appropriate leveled activity sheet for each group of learners (pages 55–57).

Access prior knowledge about historical fiction and any experiences students have had reading both nonfiction and historical fiction on the same topic. Build background on Kitty Hawk, North Carolina, and the Wright brothers' first flight.

 **Tier 1**

- **Setting:** Discuss why it helps to determine where and when a story takes place and how it influences historical fiction. Have students highlight the place and date at the top of the story; then help them locate Kitty Hawk, North Carolina, on a map.

- **Main Idea and Details:** Have students find the topic sentence of each paragraph and state the main idea. For items 2 and 3, ask students to identify the paragraph or text detail that supports each answer.

- **Author's Purpose:** For item 4, ask students to put themselves in the narrator's point of view to feel the excitement of observing a historic event.

- **Word Work:** Review *synonyms*. This activity focuses on synonyms in the form of vivid verbs that express action more precisely. You may wish to act out some of the vivid verbs.

 **Tier 2**

- **Author's Purpose:** For item 1, help students distinguish the narrator from the author. Explain that the author aims to inform readers of a historic event from the viewpoint of a girl who saw it happen.

- **Setting:** After students do item 2, talk about why the setting made sense for the Wright Brothers' work. Then help students locate Kitty Hawk, North Carolina, on a map.

- **Main Idea and Details:** Ask students to give the main idea of each paragraph. When completing items 3 and 4, students should identify the text support.

- **Word Work:** Explain that good writers choose specific descriptive verbs to help readers fully understand meaning. You may wish to assign partners to work together on this section.

 **Tier 3**

- **Author's Purpose:** After students answer item 1, compare and contrast a news account of a historic event and that event told as historical fiction. Guide them to consider audience, tone, and detail in both cases.

- **Main Idea and Details:** Have students recall finding the main idea of a paragraph and to find details to support it. Ask for volunteers to identify the main idea of each paragraph before they work on item 2 and beyond.

- **Setting:** Review the importance of setting as a literary element in historical fiction. Have students discuss what role setting plays.

- **Word Work:** You may allow students to use a thesaurus to complete this task.

# Eye-Witness to History:
## Reading Passage

### Kitty Hawk, North Carolina, 1903

I lived with my dog and my parents at the Coast Guard Station here. There really wasn't much to see or do. The area was empty except for a few scattered fishing shacks. The other locals were the mosquitoes and ticks who lived here in the summer. Overhead, gulls soared. Terns and fish hawks swooped gracefully.

Nothing much ever happened in Kitty Hawk. I spent my days hiding from Jumper in the sandy dunes or in the sea oats behind them. I flew my kite along the beach on the coast. I collected shells, lots of shells, and I built elaborate sand sculptures that Jumper always destroyed. But one day, everything about our village changed. We became famous.

It began when those two men arrived. Jumper and I watched them set up their camp and build a large shed. We saw them haul in groceries and supplies. We watched them come out of

Orville and Wilbur Wright, flying their glider as a kite at Kitty Hawk, North Carolina, 1901

© The Granger Collection

the shed with a flying machine they had built themselves. A glider, my dad called it. It had no engine. It looked flimsy and unsteady. Neither Jumper nor I had ever seen anything quite like it.

One day, we sat and watched as the men took off in their glider again and again from a huge dune called Kill Devil Hill. Jumper barked and whimpered, but I was speechless. The men would lay flat on their bellies and shimmy their hips to control the contraption. They would drift for a few seconds on the rising air currents before landing in the soft sand. They were truly flying! It was all I could do to keep Jumper with me the whole time. He had never seen such a large bird!

# Eye-Witness to History: Reading Passage

## (continued)

My father told me more about the men when I first mentioned that I had seen them. He said that they were named Orville and Wilbur Wright. These brothers came here from Dayton, Ohio, Dad said. They were bicycle mechanics who liked to tinker with things. Sometimes they invented stuff. Once, he told me, they got a little helicopter. It was a cheap toy made of fans and elastic bands. It was supposed to float in the air. He said the brothers loved that toy and soon became fascinated with flying. They came here to Kitty Hawk to experiment with flight without being disturbed or teased. Jumper and I didn't disturb or tease them at all. We just watched.

My dad told me that flying a glider wasn't very practical. But he heard that the Wright Brothers had something else in mind. He said it was a secret for now.

It was on a windy Thursday, December 17, that the secret came out. Wilbur and Orville Wright had put a motor in their machine. The two bicycle mechanics would try to raise it off the ground under its own power and fly it. Jumper and I were there when they tried this for the first time.

The contraption was outside on a track on flat ground. A wire held it there. The motor started up and sputtered for a few minutes. Then Orville released the wire. The machine began to move forward into the wind. Wilbur ran beside it, holding a wing to keep it in balance. He ran along for about forty feet when the machine began to lift itself and Orville into the air. They flew, rising up and dipping down just a few feet above the ground. Orville Wright was flying in his machine. Suddenly it darted down and crashed in the sand. Jumper howled as Orville got up and dusted himself off. We raced back home to tell Dad. They did it!

Later, my father and I read the newspaper about the flight that day. We learned that the flight covered a distance of about 120 feet. It had stayed in the air for only 12 seconds. My father understood that even this short a flight was a groundbreaking feat. He said that we had witnessed the very first time in history that a machine carrying a person rose into the air on its own power, sailed forward without losing speed, and then landed on ground no lower than the spot from which it took off.

That windy December day will stay with me all my life. The flying machine had arrived, and Jumper and I had witnessed the event. What a lucky girl I was!

 *Differentiated Activities for Teaching Key Comprehension Skills: Grades 4–6* © 2010 by Martin Lee and Marcia Miller. Scholastic Teaching Resources

Name _____   Date _____

 # Eye-Witness to History: Activity Sheet

( **Read and Understand** )  Read the passage. Then answer the questions.

**1.** Where and when does this story take place? _____

**2.** In which paragraph do we learn who the Wright Brothers were? _____

**3.** Why did the Wright Brothers choose Kitty Hawk for their work? _____

_____

**4.** Who is the narrator, and why did she write this story? _____

_____

( **Word Work: Vivid Verbs** )

A *vivid verb* is a word that shows action in an interesting way.

Gulls (flew.) ⟶ Gulls <u>soared</u>. (*Soared* is a more vivid verb for *flew*.)

Circle each verb below. Then write one or more vivid verbs used as synonyms in the story.

Jumper cried. _____

The sea birds fell. _____

The birds moved in air. _____

It went down. _____

( **Check** )  Circle the best choice.

## Which of these expresses a main idea of the story?

A.  I collected shells, lots of shells.

B.  It had stayed in the air for only 12 seconds.

C.  My dad told me that flying a glider wasn't very practical.

D.  That windy December day will stay with me all my life.

# Eye-Witness to History: Activity Sheet

**Read and Understand**  Read the passage. Then answer the questions.

**1.** Who is the narrator, and why did she write this story? _____

_____

**2.** How would you describe the setting for this story? _____

_____

**3.** What details support why Orville didn't get hurt in the crash? _____

_____

**4.** What was so special about what the Wright Brothers did that day? _____

_____

**Word Work: Vivid Verbs**

A *vivid verb* is a word that shows action in an interesting way.

Gulls (flew.) ———→ Gulls <u>soared</u>. (*Soared* is a more vivid verb for *flew.*)

Circle each verb below. Then write one or more vivid verbs used as synonyms in the story.

Jumper cried in the dunes. _____

The sea birds fell into the waves. _____

They moved with the air currents. _____

It went downward in the sand. _____

The motor ran noisily. _____

**Check**  Circle the best choice.

## Which of the following events happened first?

A. The Wright Brothers put an engine
   in their machine.

B. Orville stayed in the air for 12 seconds.

C. A flying machine crashed into
   the beach.

D. The Wright Brothers got a toy
   helicopter.

# Eye-Witness to History: Activity Sheet

**Read and Understand**  Read the passage. Then answer the questions.

**1.** Who is the narrator, and why did she write this story? _____

_____

**2.** How did the two men from Ohio change life in Kitty Hawk? _____

_____

**3** What is the main idea of Paragraph 5? _____

_____

**4.** What does it mean to be *a groundbreaking moment in history*? _____

_____

**Word Work: Vivid Verbs**

A *vivid verb* shows action in a more descriptive, precise, interesting way. Instead of *Gulls flew*, you might write *Gulls soared*, to describe exactly how they flew.

Circle the verb in each sentence. On the line that follows, write a more vivid verb.

Jumper and I ran along the beach. _____

Two strangers came to Kitty Hawk from Ohio. _____

We saw their practice flights. _____

My father told about the Wrights. _____

They put a motor in their contraption. _____

**Check**  Circle the best choice.

## Which of the following events happened first?

A. The Wright Brothers put an engine in their machine.

B. Orville stayed in the air for 12 seconds.

C. A flying machine crashed into the beach.

D. The Wright Brothers got a toy helicopter.

# Teaching *Amazing Grace, Computer Ace*

Students read a biographical sketch to learn about a leader in the field of computer science.

| Tasks | ◆ Tier 1 Below Level | ● Tier 2 On Level | ⬠ Tier 3 Above Level |
|---|---|---|---|
| Set a purpose for reading nonfiction | X | X | X |
| Identify main idea and supporting details | X | | |
| Summarize | X | X | X |
| Make connections | X | X | |
| Use context clues | X | X | X |

## Getting Started

See the tips below for introducing the lesson. Make copies of the reading passage (pages 59–60) and the appropriate leveled activity sheet for each group of learners (pages 61–63).

Access prior knowledge about biographies and biographical sketches. Briefly discuss some of the topics covered in the passage, including the historical development of computers and the branches of the U.S. military services.

 **Tier 1**

- **Purpose for Reading:** Discuss ways to set a purpose for reading: predict what the piece is about, pose questions, or seek information. Then answer item 1 together.

- **Main Idea and Details:** Have students reread Paragraph 2 to summarize Grace's characteristics of curiosity and determination. Then have them answer item 2.

- **Summarize:** Reread paragraphs 4 and 5 with students. Clarify any difficult terms or ideas. Then have students answer items 3 and 4.

- **Make Connections:** Guide students to combine what they read in the article with their own experiences. Have them compare and contrast today's computers with the Mark I for item 5.

- **Word Work:** Remind students that using context clues is an effective technique for any reading. Have them practice as they read independently.

● **Tier 2**

- **Purpose for Reading:** Explain that a biographical sketch is not a full biography but offers key events from a person's life. Challenge students to generate questions for more research.

- **Summarize:** Have students circle the paragraph that has details that will help them answer item 3.

- **Make Connections:** To help students answer items 2–4, guide them to synthesize what they read in this article, with their own prior knowledge and experience.

- **Word Work:** Discuss with students that they use context clues to establish meaning, which they can then apply to new sentences they read.

 **Tier 3**

- **Purpose for Reading:** Students interested in computers may be inspired to learn more about Grace Hopper. After they answer item 1, have them generate questions for more research.

- **Summarize:** Before students answer items 2 and 3, you may have them discuss their ideas with a partner or with the class.

- **Make Connections:** Item 4 requires students to synthesize the written materials with their prior knowledge. Have students talk about this question before they write.

- **Word Work:** Inform students that context clues can appear in the same sentence or paragraph, or anywhere else in a piece.

# Amazing Grace, Computer Ace:
## Reading Passage

### Biographical Sketch of Grace Murray Hopper
### (1906–1992)

"Either you use computers or you can't do the job," said Grace Hopper in 1986. This statement might seem obvious to us these days, but it wasn't always so. This was especially unbelievable in the early 1900s, when Grace was a girl. Electronics had not even been invented yet!

Commodore Grace Hopper in her office, 1984.

© Cynthia Johnson/Gettyimages

Grace Murray was always an inquisitive child. She was fascinated by how things work. When she was seven, she wondered what made her alarm clock ring. She took the gadget apart, but she still couldn't tell. Grace would not give up. She kept on trying—with six other alarm clocks!

Grace Murray was an eager student. She loved to learn. She earned advanced degrees in mathematics. The next year, she became a college teacher. She took pride in helping others to develop their own curiosity. She married Vincent Hopper in 1930 and became Dr. Hopper.

The United States was deeply involved in World War II in 1943, so Dr. Hopper decided to quit teaching to join the women's branch of the Navy. She was assigned to develop the new Mark I computing machine. This new device was one of the largest gadgets "Amazing Grace" had ever seen. The huge glass-enclosed mass of wires, switches, and tubes was bigger than a bus! The Mark I stored data and did math very quickly. Grace saw the future in machines like this one. She was excited to be part of it. Hopper and her team of other mathematicians and engineers soon moved onto the Mark II, a newer, more powerful model.

A 1964 IBM System 360 computer, including a typewriter-like machine which was used to communicate with the huge mainframe behind it

People today know that computers can misbehave. Computer problems are called "bugs." It was Dr. Hopper who made this term popular. One day, the Mark II simply stopped working. Amazing Grace took it apart to figure out the problem. To her surprise, she saw a dead moth stuck between two contacts! The moth blocked the electricity from moving through the circuit. Hopper gently removed the moth and taped it into her lab book. She wrote, "First actual case of a bug being found." To this day, experts "debug" when they hunt down and fix a computer malfunction.

Grace Hopper has been called the "mother of computing." This pioneer achieved many firsts in her career. She was the first woman to develop programs for early computers. She was the first person to be named Computer Science Man of the Year (yes, "man"!). She was the oldest officer on active duty in the Navy when she retired at age eighty.

Grace Murray Hopper lived by a simple motto: "Dare and do." Four years after her death, the Navy found a special way to honor her. They launched a new ship named *USS Hopper* in 1996. The *Amazing Grace* is one of the very few U.S. military vessels named for a woman. In a way, Hopper continues to inspire others to dare and do.

# Amazing Grace, Computer Ace: Activity Sheet

**Read and Understand**  Read the passage. Then answer the questions.

**1.** What is your purpose for reading this piece? _____

_____

**2.** How did young Grace show an early interest in science? _____

_____

**3.** In one sentence, summarize Grace's work during World War II. _____

_____

**4.** Where does the term "debug" come from? _____

_____

**5.** What is one of the biggest differences between modern computers and the Mark I?

_____

**Word Work: Context Clues**

Find and circle in the passage the five words below. Then look for clues to each meaning. Use a highlighter to underline clues that help you.

inquisitive          mass          malfunction

motto          launched

**Check**  Circle the best choice.

## Why was Grace Hopper known as "Amazing Grace"?

A. She was a brave member of the Navy.

B. She had the same name as a Navy ship.

C. She was a pioneer in modern computer science.

D. She was a great mathematician.

# ● Amazing Grace, Computer Ace: Activity Sheet

**Read and Understand**   Read the passage. Then answer the questions.

**1.** What is your purpose for reading this piece? _____

_____

**2.** Why did Grace quit teaching in 1943? _____

_____

**3** In one sentence, summarize Grace's work during World War II. _____

_____

**4.** Do you think Grace Hopper was right about computers? Explain. _____

_____

**Word Work: Context Clues**

Find and circle in the passage the four words below. Use context clues to determine their meaning. Then write each word in the sentence below where it makes sense.

**mass    malfunction    motto    launched**

- ◉   The accident was caused by a _____ of the brakes.

- ◉   The government _____ a new project to improve education.

- ◉   The Boy Scouts' _____ is "Be prepared."

- ◉   Ayers Rock is the largest sandstone _____ in Australia.

**Check**   Circle the best choice.

**Which statement best summarizes Grace Murray Hopper's early life?**

A. She showed an early love for clocks.

B. She followed her natural curiosity and deep love of learning.

C. She set out to invent the modern computer.

D. She longed to become professor.

# Amazing Grace, Computer Ace: Activity Sheet

**Read and Understand**  Read the passage. Then answer the questions.

**1.** What is your purpose for reading this piece? _____

_____

**2.** In one sentence, summarize Grace as a young girl. _____

_____

**3.** In one sentence, summarize Grace's work during World War II. _____

_____

**4.** In what ways did Grace Hopper live up to her motto? _____

_____

**Word Work: Context Clues**

In the passage, find and circle the four words listed below. Look for clues to each meaning. Then write an original sentence using each word that hints at its meaning.

inquisitive_____

mass _____

malfunction _____

motto _____

**Check**  Circle the best choice.

## Why did Dr. Hopper decide to quit teaching mathematics in 1943?

A.  She wanted to become a Navy officer.

B.  She wanted to use her skills to help the war effort.

C.  She wanted to build a new computer.

D.  She was tired of teaching math.

# Teaching **Two Poems**

**Skills:**
- Recognizing figurative language
- Comparing and contrasting

Students read two different poems that use figurative language to describe nature.

| Tasks | Tier 1 Below Level | Tier 2 On Level | Tier 3 Above Level |
|---|---|---|---|
| Recognize metaphor and personification | X | X | X |
| Examine rhyme patterns | | X | X |
| Compare and contrast | | X | X |
| Use contractions | X | | |
| Use the past tense of irregular verbs | | X | X |

## Getting Started

See the tips below for introducing the lesson. Make copies of the reading passage (page 65) and the appropriate leveled activity sheet for each group of learners (pages 66–68).

Access prior knowledge about poetry. Build background on similes, metaphors, personification, and other forms of figurative language.

## Tier 1

- **Figurative Language:** Explain that poets use a *metaphor* as a way to describe one thing by calling it something else. Show images of colorful gypsy attire to give them a sense of the personification "gypsy queen." Write *personification* on the board and circle *person* in it. Explain that it is making a non-human thing act like a person. For instance, the sun can't really use a crayon, but that's how the poet describes how the sky turns red. Read aloud the poems slowly. Ask students to visualize each. Help them answer items 1-4.

- **Vocabulary:** Clarify that *tripping* in "October" means stepping lightly, not stumbling.

- **Word Work:** Describe an *apostrophe* as a punctuation mark that looks like a floating comma. Circle apostrophes in common contractions, such as *I'm* or *can't*. Then help students fill in the table. Point out contractions as they occur in other texts.

## Tier 2

- **Figurative Language:** Remind students that poets use *metaphors* to describe one thing as something else and *personification* to have a non-human thing act as a person might. Explain that "October is a gypsy queen" is a metaphor the poet uses as a fresh way to describe the month. Identify personification in "Green-Apple Morning." As students read the poems, have them visualize what the poet's words evoke.

- **Compare and Contrast:** For item 3, help students find the rhyme pattern. Use ABCB to show that the 2nd and 4th lines rhyme but the 1st and 3rd lines do not. Then have students describe the rhyme pattern in "Green-Apple Morning."

- **Word Work:** Use examples of irregular past-tense verbs from "Green-Apple Morning": *stood* (for *stand*) and *was* (for *is*).

## Tier 3

- **Figurative Language:** Ask students to identify and explain metaphors and personification in each poem before doing items 1–3. Have them reread the poems to clarify how this figurative language creates fresh images of autumn and of summer mornings.

- **Compare and Contrast:** For item 4, discuss how the two poems look different, yet both use the ABCB rhyme pattern. Have students compare and contrast the mood of each poem.

- **Word Work:** Extend by listing other irregular past-tense verbs: build/built, light/lit, creep/crept.

**Skills:**
• Recognizing figurative language
• Comparing and contrasting

# Two Poems:
## Reading Passage

Some poets gather ideas from nature. Read each poem.
Pay attention to the images that come into your mind.

## October
by Winifred C. Marshall

October is a gypsy queen
In dress of red and gold.
She sleeps beneath the silver moon
When nights are crisp and cold.

The meadows flame with color now,
Which once were cool and green.
Wild asters and the goldenrod
Bow low to greet their queen.

## Green-Apple Morning
by Mary Graham Bond

It's a green-apple morning,
Polished with sun,
And here in the orchard
Mist is spun.
The sun's red crayon
Paints the hill
While orchard trees stand
Picture-still.
I run to the end of
This new day,
And the green-apple morning
Slips away.

# Two Poems: Activity Sheet

( **Read and Understand** )  Read the passage. Then answer the questions.

**1.** Who is the "she" in the poem "October"? _____

**2.** What does the "dress of red and gold" stand for? _____

_____

**3.** What color is the daybreak in the poem "Green-Apple Morning?" _____

**4.** In what season is "Green-Apple Morning"? _____

   Why do you think so? _____

_____

( **Word Work: Contractions** )

Read each contraction below. Circle the apostrophe. Then write the words that the contraction is made from. Underline the letter(s) not in the contraction.

| Contraction | Long Form |
|:-----------:|:---------:|
| I've | I have |
| couldn't | |
| you're | |
| she'll | |
| haven't | |

( **Check** )  Circle the best choice.

## What made the color of the meadow change?

A.  the sun's red crayon

B.  the silver moon

C.  the morning mist

D.  the cold crisp weather

Name _____    Date _____

 # Two Poems: Activity Sheet

**Read and Understand** ) Read the passage. Then answer the questions.

**1.** Why do you think the poet describes October as a "gypsy queen"? _____

_____

**2.** What really makes the asters and goldenrod bow? _____

_____

**3.** Describe the rhyme pattern in "October." _____

_____

**4.** What weather words could describe the day in "Green-Apple Morning"? _____

_____

**Word Work: Irregular Past Tense** )

Some verbs do not form the past tense with *-d* or *-ed*.
*Irregular* verbs change form in other ways.

Rapunzel *spun* straw
into gold.

*Spun* is the past tense
of spin.

Read each phrase in the
table. Notice the irregular
past-tense verb. Then write
the present tense of each.

| Irregular Verb | Present-Tense Verb |
|---|---|
| October <u>was</u>… | October _____ |
| She <u>slept</u>… | She _____ |
| Meadows <u>were</u>… | Meadows _____ |
| Trees <u>stood</u>… | Trees _____ |
| I <u>ran</u>… | I _____ |

**Check** )

Circle the best choice.
**What made the color of the meadow change?**

A.  the sun's red crayon            C.  the morning mist

B.  the wild asters                 D.  the cold crisp weather

# ⬠ Two Poems: Activity Sheet

**( Read and Understand )** Read the passage. Then answer the questions.

**1.** Why do you think the poet describes October as a "gypsy queen"? _____

_____

**2.** In what season is the poem "Green-Apple Morning" set? _____

Why do you think so? _____

**3.** What happens after the speaker runs in "Green-Apple Morning"? _____

_____

**4.** Compare and contrast the rhyme pattern in the two poems. _____

_____

**( Word Work: Irregular Past Tense )**

Irregular verbs do not form the past tense with *-d* or *-ed*. For example, *spin* becomes *spun*. Circle the irregular verb in each sentence. Rewrite the sentence using the past-tense irregular verb.

| Present Tense | Past Tense |
|---|---|
| We arise early. | |
| You become strong. | |
| He bites an apple. | |
| Autumn winds blow. | |
| I catch the ball. | |

**( Check )** Circle the best choice.

## Which quotation is a metaphor?

A. Autumn leaves come sifting down.

B. Orchard trees stand picture-still.

C. I run to the end of this new day.

D. October is a gypsy queen.

# Teaching
# Gliding Through the Air

**Skills:**
- Recognizing author's point of view
- Identifying text features
- Recognizing cause-and-effect relationships

Students read a humorous story about an adventure 2500 feet above the ground.

| Tasks | Tier 1 Below Level | Tier 2 On Level | Tier 3 Above Level |
|---|---|---|---|
| Recognize author's point of view | X | X | X |
| Identify text features | X | X | X |
| Recognize cause-and-effect relationships | X | X | X |
| Use hyphenated words as modifiers | X | | |
| Suffix *-meter* | | X | X |

## Getting Started

See the tips below for introducing the lesson. Make copies of the reading passage (pages 70–71) and the appropriate leveled activity sheet for each group of learners (pages 72–74).

Access prior knowledge about different kinds of small planes. Discuss styles of humor, including the use of irony and exaggeration in writing. Also review the use of italics to present a narrator's inner voice.

 ## Tier 1

- **Author's Point of View:** Guide a discussion about each of the three characters in the story. Have students highlight and describe examples of Ted's and Carl's senses of humor.

- **Cause and Effect:** After discussing item 2, ask students to point out text details to explain why Ted seems to be so scared. Talk about why people may turn to humor in scary situations. Ask: *Does Ted really think of Max as a former friend?* Talk about why.

- **Text Features:** For item 3, explain that a narrator's *inner voice* is what he or she is thinking but not saying aloud.

- **Word Work:** Help students to list other hyphenated modifiers. Get started by suggesting, such as *color-coded, high-tech,* or *tree-lined.*

 ## Tier 2

- **Author's Point of View:** For item 1, have students identify specific text details that reveal which character is narrating.

- **Text Features:** For item 2, explain that a narrator's *inner voice* is what he/she is thinking but not saying aloud.

- **Cause and Effect:** For item 4, ask, *How did Ted really feel about his friend Max and about the glider flight itself? What do you think about the way Ted described the flight to others?* You may want to discuss the meaning of *irony* as a way of communicating by using words that mean the opposite of what you really think and ask students to cite examples in the story.

- **Word Work:** Ask students to brainstorm other words with this suffix.

 ## Tier 3

- **Author's Point of View:** Ask students to recall and share times when they themselves thought one thing but said another. Discuss the concept of a narrator's inner voice and the use of italics to show it.

- **Cause and Effect:** For item 3, ask, *Why do you think Carl jokes about his flying credentials?* For item 4, inform students that *irony* is a way of communicating by using words that mean the opposite of what you really think. Have students identify other examples of irony in the story.

- **Word Work:** Have students brainstorm other words with this suffix and then recall other suffixes they know and words that have them.

**Skills:**
- Recognizing author's point of view
- Identifying text features
- Recognizing cause-and-effect relationships

# Gliding Through the Air

## Reading Passage

"I'm Captain Carl. Are you two dudes strapped in tight?" the glider pilot asked without turning to look at us. "Are you ready for the thrill of your lives?"

When he was sure that we were his captives, he described the machine in which we were trapped. He talked about its parts and compared them to those of a small airplane with an engine. "We've got the same parts that planes do—just no engine. Fiberglass construction, sleek, smooth design. Got a couple of pedals down on the floor. Got a 55-foot wingspan and very long, thin wings. Moveable parts of the wings control our direction. We go up and down with the help of this variometer here. It tells us what the air currents are up to. A quick-release mechanism in the nose lets us loose after we've been towed to altitude. Any questions before take-off?"

*Yeah, I have questions like . . .* "How long will this thrill ride take?" *and* "Will I survive?" As my mind raced, I began to sweat.

"Yes, I have a question, sir. Um, what kind of training have you had?"

That got a chuckle from Captain Carl. "Oh, tons of training, mostly hang gliding and bungee jumping. Some surfing, too. I've learned a lot over the weeks," he said. "Okay. Hang tight, dudes. Here we go!"

*Oh, no! Time to hope and trust and have faith.* I squeezed my eyes shut.

The engine in the small plane ahead of us roared. We felt the tow line tighten. Both aircraft began to move down the runway. Within seconds, the plane and the glider were aloft. Within moments, we were 2,500 feet above the lower ridges of a mountain range.

"Cool beans! Looks like we have us a nice thermal," Captain Carl said as he hit the quick release. Suddenly, we were freed from the tow plane. Silence! So began our non-powered flight. "Now just relax and enjoy the ride," he added, turning slightly toward us and winking.

*Relax? Enjoy? Are you nuts?*

# Gliding Through the Air: Reading Passage
## (continued)

There I was, strapped into a tiny seat tucked behind the cockpit and the top of Carl's head. He was reclining. I was sitting up, stiff as iron. My left hand pressed against the clear, curved window above me. My right gripped my seat as tightly as it could. I was panicky. How could I have let that airhead crammed in next to me talk me into this? I refer to my giddy co-passenger and (former!) friend Max. Yuck—Max was now drooling with delight.

"Isn't this amazing, Ted?" he said, beaming at me. "Whoa! Check out those mountains we're heading for. Wee-hah!"

*We're going to die. I know we're going to die.*

"Dudes! We're now totally flying like birds do," Captain Carl exclaimed. "Awesome, right?" he said as he steered the glider up and away from certain death. He used the rising air to lift us over the sheer wall that only I seemed to fear.

Max was having the time of his life. "How cool is this, Tedster? I'm like pumped, so wow!"

I forced a grin, but "so wow" was not exactly my point of view. "Scared spitless" was more like it. *If this is what "flying like birds" is like, I guess birds must be terrified and can't wait to land.*

After more stomach-churning dips and sky-high climbs, Captain Carl raised the spoilers atop the wings in order to bring us down to earth. "Our landing gear? It's one wheel mounted below the cockpit," Carl announced. "We've got another little wheel under the tail to keep it from scraping the ground. My plan is to keep both wing tips in the air. Let's see if I can. Wish me luck!"

*Luck?*

Again, I shut my eyes and held my breath. To my vast relief, we landed safely. Still, it felt like riding a skateboard at warp speed down stairs. I was still shaking when Carl brought the glider to a full stop. It was over. I lived. We all lived.

In the weeks that followed, I told everybody about my airborne adventure. I dramatically described the excitement and thrills. I gushed about the stunning views. It was obvious that I'd had a terrific time. But you and I know that the fun started long after the event ended. One day, I'll recall my harrowing flight as a merry joyride. I'm sure that's how Max remembers it.

Name _____   Date _____

# ◆ Gliding Through the Air: Activity Sheet

**Read and Understand**  Read the passage. Then answer the questions.

**1.** What is the name of the person who tells the story? _____

**2.** How would you describe the narrator during the flight? Explain. _____

_____

**3.** Who is thinking the words and sentences in *italics?* _____

Are these words spoken out loud? _____

**4.** Why does Ted describe Max as a "former" friend? _____

_____

**Word Work: Hyphens in Modifiers**

Hyphens sometimes connect words that *modify,* or describe other words.

the **world-famous** pilot

a **long-lost** friend

The story has *four* examples of modifiers with hyphens. Find all four. Write each in the table. Then write the word it describes.

| Hyphenated Words | Word Described |
|---|---|
|  |  |
|  |  |
|  |  |
|  |  |

**Check**  Circle the best choice.

**Which is something Ted really believed?**

A. Max was very much enjoying himself.

B. Birds are scared to fly and can't wait to land.

C. Carl's flight training consisted of hang gliding and bungee jumping.

D. He was going to die on this flight.

# ⬤ Gliding Through the Air: Activity Sheet

**( Read and Understand )** Read the passage. Then answer the questions.

**1.** How does Ted use humor to describe the flight and his feelings? _____

_____

**2.** Why do some words and sentences appear in *italics*? Explain. _____

_____

**3.** How does Captain Carl show that he has a sense of humor? _____

_____

**4.** Why did Ted tell people that he loved his glider flight? _____

_____

**( Word Work: Suffix: -meter )**

The suffix *-meter* means "a device for measuring." A glider pilot uses a *variometer* to measure air currents. Write the letter of each tool beside what it does.

A. barometer           _____ tool for measuring temperature

B. chronometer         _____ tool for measuring how fast

C. hydrometer          _____ tool for measuring air pressure

D. speedometer         _____ tool for measuring time accurately

E. thermometer         _____ tool for measuring liquid density

**( Check )** Circle the best choice.

## Which is something Ted really believed?

A. Max was very much enjoying himself.

B. Birds are terrified of flight and can't wait to land.

C. Max was no longer his friend.

D. He was going to die on that flight.

# Gliding Through the Air: Activity Sheet

**Read and Understand** Read the passage. Then answer the questions.

**1.** How does Ted use humor to describe the flight and his feelings? _____

_____

**2.** Why do some of the words and sentences appear in *italics*? _____

What do they reveal about Ted? _____

**3.** Who else in the story reveals a sense of humor? Explain. _____

_____

**4.** How does the final paragraph show Ted's sense of irony? _____

_____

**Word Work: Suffix: -meter**

The suffix *-meter* means "a device for measuring." A glider pilot uses a *variometer* to measure air currents. Write the letter of each tool beside what it does.

A. barometer         _____ tool for measuring temperature

B. chronometer       _____ tool for measuring how fast

C. hydrometer        _____ tool for measuring air pressure

D. speedometer       _____ tool for measuring time accurately

E. thermometer       _____ tool for measuring liquid density

**Check** Circle the best choice.

## Which is a reliable comment Ted could make about a glider flight?

A. Glider pilots train by hang gliding, bungee jumping, and surfing.

B. You are sure to die during the experience.

C. You will have the time of your life.

D. You will dip, soar, and glide like a bird.

# Reading Response Prompts

**How to Train a Puppy**
**Not to Jump**

◆ **Why Train?**

Write a paragraph explaining why it is a bad idea to let puppies jump up on people.

● **To the Puppy**

Write a letter from a dog owner to its puppy, explaining the choice of this training method.

⬟ **Causes and Effects**

Make a cause-and-effect T-chart for each of the five training steps.

---

**Freddy's E-Mail**

◆ **Write Back!**

Pretend you are Squirt. Write back to Freddy. What questions might Squirt ask? Write about what's been happening at home.

● **Dr. Chen's Viewpoint**

Pretend you are Dr. Chen. Write an e-mail from her point of view. Express her interest in creating a community dog run.

⬟ **Community Project**

Consider the needs of your community. Write an e-mail about a service project that leaders and citizens might do together. Explain what, where, why, and how.

---

**A Family Movie Classic**

◆ **Verbal Review**

Plan and practice an oral review of a film, concert, or TV show within 1-minute. Tell what was good and bad about it. End with your recommendation.

● **Review a Film**

Write a review of a movie you have seen. Give facts and opinions to support why you liked or disliked it. End with your recommendation.

⬟ **Review a Review!**

Research real reviews of *The Wizard of Oz* online or in books at the library. Pick one to evaluate. Tell why you agree or disagree with the review.

---

**Is That You, Jack?**

◆ **Fact vs. Fiction**

Science fiction blends facts and fiction. Look back at the story. Use two colors of highlighter pens. Highlight science facts in one color. Highlight pure fiction in another color.

● **Was That Jack?**

Think about the title and how it fits this story. Who is asking the question? Why? How did that odd encounter affect the narrator? Explain your ideas.

⬟ **Open Your Mind**

Pretend you are a reporter who listened to the narrator's story with an open mind. Write an article in which you report the events as you heard them.

---

**Shades of Meaning**

◆ **Concept Web**

Make a concept web to show the different reasons why people wear sunglasses.

● **To Shade or Not**

Is it a good idea to wear sunglasses? Write a paragraph explaining why or why not. Support your view with details from the passage.

⬟ **Buy These Shades**

Write an advertisement for sunglasses directed to an audience of twelve-year-old kids.

---

**Two Rice Cakes**

◆ **Point of View**

Imagine that you were the son who became the king at the end of the story. Retell the tale from this character's point of view.

● **Compare and Contrast**

Read another folktale from Vietnam or any Asian country. Compare and contrast the two folktales. Write a review that explains which one you prefer and why.

⬟ **Rice**

Do research at the library and online to learn how rice is grown. Present your findings as a report or as an informational poster.

# Reading Response Prompts

## School Schedule Debate

**◆ Debate Chart**

Make a T-chart. List Karen's key arguments in one column and Hassan's key arguments in the other.

**● Debate Blog**

Pretend you are a blogger and you are covering the debate for an online site. Write your opinion of each debater's argument.

**⬠ Another Opinion**

Decide which debater you support. Add your opinions and ideas to that person's argument in a speech.

## The Navajo Code Talkers

**◆ Review the Reasons**

List the reasons that the Navajo Code Talkers were so successful.

**● Medal of Honor**

Write a paragraph to explain why you think the Code Talkers did or did not deserve their Congressional Medals of Honor.

**⬠ War Reporter**

Pretend you are a war reporter in World War II. You cover a battle in which the Code Talkers play a part. Write an article describing what you saw and heard.

## Eye-Witness to History

**◆ Taking Notes**

What if you had to write a report about what the Wright Brothers did at Kitty Hawk. Take notes. Write the facts: who, what, when, where, why, and how.

**● Sensory Details**

Pretend you are the narrator. Describe how it might have felt watching the Wright Brothers on that windy December day. Use sensory details (sight, sound, taste, touch, smell) to describe the scene.

**⬠ Orville's Thoughts**

Imagine yourself as Orville Wright on December 17, 1903. Write the thoughts that might have been going through your mind as you tried to fly. Use details from the passage to guide you.

## Amazing Grace, Computer Ace

**◆ Ace It!**

"Ace" is a slang term for a person who is extremely good at something. For instance, a flying ace is an excellent pilot. List five people who you think are aces at something.

**● Tinkering**

Think back on a time when you or someone you know tried to figure out how to fix something or solve a problem. Maybe this person found the solution, but maybe not. Write about the event.

**⬠ My Motto**

Think about your goals for your life. Make up a short motto that summarizes these goals and sets forth an idea to live by. Explain your choice.

## Two Poems

**◆ Read and Recite**

Practice reading the poems aloud. Say each line clearly and read with emotion. When you are ready, read the poems to classmates. Or see if you can memorize and recite them.

**● Color Metaphors**

Make up a metaphor for six different colors. For example, "Pink is a bubble-gum tree" and "Gray is a cloud of sadness." Follow up by writing a stanza for one of the colors.

**⬠ Monthly Metaphors**

Think about a metaphor for each month. For example, "January is an ice cave." List each metaphor in calendar order. Then write one stanza for each month.

## Gliding Through the Air

**◆ Glider Cartoon**

Create a cartoon that shows a scene from this story. Include a caption or voice bubbles.

**● Thanks, Captain**

Write a note from Ted to Captain Carl, sincerely thanking him for the experience of a glider flight. Try to sound like Ted might sound.

**⬠ Max's Thoughts**

The words in italics give Ted's inner thoughts. Write a parallel set of inner thoughts that Max might have had at each moment.

# Answer Key

## How to Train a Puppy Not to Jump

**Tier 1, page 11: Read and Understand:** 1. how to teach a puppy not to jump 2. to show the correct order to do the steps 3. Steps 1 and 2 4. It thinks you want to play; **Word Work:** li_g_ht _g_host _k_now; _k_nit ta_l_k s_c_ene; si_g_n thum_b_; _t_wo _g_uard i_s_land; **Check:** C

**Tier 2, page 12: Read and Understand:** 1. how to train a puppy not to jump 2. The puppy will learn better with someone calm. 3. to show the correct order to do them in 4. "not to push your dog off"; **Word Work:** smart, scare, visitor, strike, easily; **Check:** B

**Tier 3, page 13: Read and Understand:** 1. how to train a puppy not to jump 2. There are headings, a bulleted list for items needed, a numbered list of steps to follow. 3. It encourages the pup to jump up because it thinks the guest is playing. 4. as often as needed until its behavior improves; **Word Work:** smart, stay, visitor, frightens, immediately; **Check:** B

## Freddy's E-mail

**Tier 1, page 16: Read and Understand:** 1. It briefly summarizes the e-mail. 2. vacant 3. The project was Dr. Chen's idea, and she made it happen. 4. *Students should put a star next to the text: First, we raked the ground clean and smooth. Then we spread out the wood chips evenly everywhere.* 5. The class "carpeted" the dog run; **Word Work:** space: area, unlimited place beyond earth, distance apart; fence: kind of boundary, fight with a sword; **Check:** A

**Tier 2, page 17: Read and Understand:** 1. Squirt is Freddy's little brother or sister. *Students should put a star next to:* Say hi to Mom and Dad *and* And get some time away from you, Squirt! 2. He misses Squirt; he wants to share his excitement. 3. donated 4. Many groups work at the same time on different jobs. 5. Sample answer: Making a difference; **Word Work:** stumble; space: area, unlimited place beyond earth, distance apart; fence: kind of boundary, fight with a sword; sheds: storage shelters, lets drop, gets rid of; **Check:** D

**Tier 3, page 18: Read and Understand:** 1. *Sample answer: Volunteering to help your community can be fun and bring pride.* 2. He and his class help prepare the new dog run. 3. They get a safe, enclosed space where dogs can run free and play together. 4. The project moved ahead; many people, organizations, and companies took part. 5. frisky; **Word Work:** Fenced-in, inside a fenced area; off-leash, without wearing a leash; chain-link, links made of chain attached together to make a fence; two-gate, with two separate gates; last-night, happening on the last night; **Check:** D

## A Family Movie Classic

**Tier 1, page 21: Read and Understand:** 1. *Check that students circle sentences that endorse the film.* 2. *Check that students list two facts, such as:* It came out in 1939; it begins in black and white; first audiences saw it in movie theaters; it won for best music in a film. 3. There are scary parts, but they don't last long and aren't like those horror films. 4. They are corny, but they work. **Word Work:** rain/bow; day/dreams; sound/track; every/one; **Check:** A

**Tier 2, page 22: Read and Understand:** 1. *Check that students list two facts, such as:* It came out in 1939; it begins in black and white; first audiences saw it in movie theaters; it won for best music in a film. 2. *Check that students list two opinions, such as:* I bet it is as exciting to new audiences today as it was back then; Even the soundtrack fits just right! I do feel that the acting, special effects, and dialogue are corny, but they still work. 3. They are actual lines from the movie and its song lyrics. 4. There are favorable reviews of the story, acting, music, and overall effectiveness of the film. **Word Work:** farm/house, house on a farm; rain/bow, arc of colors in the sky; day/dreams, ideas you think about while awake; sound/track, all the background music in a film; every/one, all people; **Check:** A

**Tier 3, page 23: Read and Understand:** 1. It introduces readers to the reviewer's point of view. 2. *Check that students list one fact, such as:* It came out in 1939; it begins in black and white; first audiences saw it in movie theaters; it won for best music in a film; *Check that students list one opinion, such as:* I bet it is as exciting to new audiences today as it was back then; Even the soundtrack fits just right! I do feel that the acting, special effects, and dialogue are corny, but they still work. 3. There are favorable reviews of the story, acting, music, and overall effectiveness of the film. 4. They are actual lines from the movie and its song lyrics. **Word Work:** ending: closing, beginning; recall: remember, forget; corny: old-fashioned, original; comforting: calming, upsetting, depressing; **Check:** D

# Answer Key (continued)

## Is That You, Jack?

**Tier 1, page 27: Read and Understand:** 1. Jack moved onto the narrator's street when they were kids, in sixth grade 2. They kept to themselves. They spoke differently. 3. *Students should use three of the following words: smart, honest, warm-hearted, interesting, and modest.* 4. Jack was still a boy while the narrator was an adult. 5. Maybe he really was from Mars; **Word Work:** *image:* a picture or idea; *imagine:* to make up a picture or idea; *imagination:* the ability to make up a picture or idea in your mind; **Check:** A

**Tier 2, page 28: Read and Understand:** 1. He knows that the story sounds crazy, even though he believes that it's true. 2. They were scientists and researchers, so they probably used those tools and instruments for their work. 3. He was attending an astronomy conference. 4. They looked as they had decades earlier. **Word Work:** astronomers, hydrofoil, lecture, dialogue; **Check:** A

**Tier 3, page 29: Read and Understand:** 1. *Sample answers: Maybe they were busy with work; maybe they didn't feel welcome in the neighborhood; maybe they had secrets to hide.* 2. Possible answer: He is simply answering the questions truthfully. 3. The narrator writes as an adult, sharing childhood memories about an old friend who he thinks he recently saw many years later. He talks about having grown up to be a scientist. 4. *Sample answers: Jack really was from Mars, where people don't age; the narrator was wrong—it wasn't Jack; Jack was a robot.* **Word Work:** astronomers: scientists who study the stars; hydrofoil: special kind of fast boat; lecture: to read to a group; dialogue: speech between two or more people; universe: everything in space; **Check:** A

## Shades of Meaning

**Tier 1, page 32: Read and Understand:** 1. China 2. shades, dark glasses, sunnies, coolers 3. 1929; 4. swimming, skiing, cycling, mountain climbing; 5. celebrities wore them; **Word Work:** in a silent way, in a recent way, in a serious way, in a sad way; **Check:** D

**Tier 2, page 33: Read and Understand:** 1. *Possible answer: I expect to learn about the history and uses of sunglasses.* 2. in China, about 1,000 years ago 3. India 4. It is only recently that sunglasses have became commonly worn. 5. in chronological order; **Word Work:** silently; recently; humbly; happily; **Check:** C

**Tier 3, page 34: Read and Understand:** 1. *Possible answer: I expect to learn about the history and uses of sunglasses.* 2. to hide what they were thinking 3. People wear sunglasses for many reasons 4. *Possible answer: They believe that fashion-conscious people will want and pay for designer labels on sunglasses since they are popular.* 5. in chronological order; **Word Work:** Students' sentences should include *silently, recently, humbly, happily;* **Check:** B

## Two Rice Cakes

**Tier 1, page 37: Read and Understand:** 1. He wanted to pick an heir, but he had twenty-two sons. 2. He was just a farmer; he didn't begin the quest right away but returned to his farm. 3. They thought they were too modest and not special or different enough. 4. Tiet-Lieu grew the rice himself and made the cakes with the help of his family; the rice cakes were the shapes of the sky and earth. **Word Work:** heir/air; prince/prints; sent/scent; flour/flower; **Check:** D

**Tier 2, page 38: Read and Understand:** 1. He hoped to find which of his sons truly understood and appreciated the land he would one day rule. 2. He was just a farmer; he didn't begin the quest right away but returned to his farm. 3. He was impressed that Tiet-Lieu used the rice he'd grown himself and made the cakes with the help of his entire family. 4. They are round like the sky and square like the earth; **Word Work:** prince/prints; scent/sent/cent; flour/flower; **Check:** B

**Tier 3, page 39: Read and Understand:** 1. He hoped to find which of his sons truly understand and appreciated the land he would one day rule. 2. They thought they were too modest, not special or different enough. 3. They are round like the sky and square like the earth. 4. *Possible answers: The values of family, respect for the land, honor, obedience, politeness, tradition;* **Word Work:** prince, son of a king; flour, ground-up grain; turn, chance; scent, fragrance, odor; **Check:** B

# Answer Key *(continued)*

## School Schedule Debate

**Tier 1, page 43: Read and Understand:** 1. Hassan 2. She says that teachers need more time to teach and would welcome the extra pay. 3. Parents will appreciate that their children will learn more if they are in school longer. 4. He describes the large amount of time his older brother spends on school activities. **Word Work:** few; advanced; shorten; disagree; worse; **Check:** B

**Tier 2, page 44: Read and Understand:** 1. Hassan 2. Both debaters think so. 3. They will have more time for key subjects and subjects they like, with less homework and more time for fun. 4. They can equip teachers with better texts and give fewer but better tests. 5. Both agree that they like their own school, but that many schools need improvement; that more money needs to be spent; **Word Work:** shorter; completely; basic; group; **Check:** B

**Tier 3, page 45: Read and Understand:** 1. Students need to put in more effort and so must teachers. 2. She says both will appreciate the additional time available for subjects students enjoy. 3. Both agree that they like their school, but that many schools need improvement. They both feel that more money needs to be spent. 4. *Answers will vary; Check that students provide support.* **Word Work:** shorter; completely; basic; group; core; **Check:** B

## The Navajo Code Talkers

**Tier 1, page 49: Read and Understand:** 1. The Japanese, who we were fighting, had cracked other codes used by the U.S. 2. He suggested using the Navajo language as a new secret code. 3. It was very quick to use in practice, and it was never broken. 4. to highlight the important wartime contribution made by the Navajo code talkers; **Word Work:** unknown/not known; dishonest/not honest; disloyal/not loyal; uncommon/not common; **Check:** B

**Tier 2, page 50: Read and Understand:** 1. *Possible answer: to share the wartime contribution made by the code talkers; to inform about one aspect of World War II.* 2. The Japanese had cracked the American codes and knew all their plans, so the Americans used the Navajo language as a new secret code. 3. Messages could be sent quickly and safely; military plans once again could remain secret. 4. The Navajo Code Talkers proved to be of great military value; their efforts saved many lives. **Word Work:** unfamiliar; disrupt; disqualify; unknown; **Check:** B

**Tier 3, page 51: Read and Understand:** 1. *Possible answer: to share the contribution to our country made by the code talkers; to inform about one aspect of World War II.* 2. The American army used a new unbreakable code so that the Japanese could not discover its plans. 3. They are not written languages and are spoken by few people. 4. *Possible answer: Using secrecy and codes keep plans unknown to the enemy and disrupt their own plans.* **Word Work:** recruit; command; force; ambush; **Check:** C

## Eye-Witness to History

**Tier 1, page 55: Read and Understand:** 1. The story takes place in Kitty Hawk, North Carolina, in 1903. 2. Paragraph 5 3. It was quiet, deserted, wide open, and had soft ground. 4. A girl living in Kitty Hawk, when the Wright Brothers made their historic flight, wanted to tell about being an eye-witness. **Word Work:** whimpered, howled; swooped, dipped down; sailed, soared; darted, crashed; **Check:** D

**Tier 2, page 56: Read and Understand:** 1. A girl living in Kitty Hawk, North Carolina, when the Wright Brothers made their historic flight; she wanted to tell about being an eye-witness. 2. The story takes place in Kitty Hawk, North Carolina, in 1903. It seems like it was a quiet beach town. 3. The plane was just a few feet off the ground, and the sandy ground was soft. 4. Their flying machine took off and landed using its own power. It was the world's first powered airplane flight; **Word Work:** cried: whimpered, howled; fell: swooped, dipped down; moved: sailed, soared; went: darted, crashed; ran: sputtered; **Check:** D

**Tier 3, page 57: Read and Understand:** 1. A girl living in Kitty Hawk, North Carolina, when the Wright Brothers made their historic flight; she wanted to tell about being an eye-witness. 2. After they successfully flew their flying machine, Kitty Hawk changed from an unknown town to a famous one. 3. The Wright Brothers came from Ohio to Kitty Hawk to test their ideas about flying. 4. It's such an important event that things that come afterwards will never be the same. **Word Work:** ran: cavorted, scampered; came: moved, relocated; saw: observed, spied on; told: explained, gossiped, reported; put: installed, rigged up, mounted; **Check:** D

# Answer Key *(continued)*

## Amazing Grace, Computer Ace

**Tier 1, page 61: Read and Understand**: 1. *Possible answer:* To find out who "Amazing Grace" was and how she got her nickname 2. She was fascinated by how things worked and took things apart to figure them out. 3. *Possible answer:* She worked with other mathematicians and engineers to develop modern computing machines for the Navy. 4. It comes from the time an actual bug (a moth) got stuck in a computer and stopped it from working. 5. Modern computers can be very small while the Mark I was as big as a bus. **Word Work:** *Check students' highlighting in the passage*; **Check:** C

**Tier 2, page 62: Read and Understand**: 1. *Possible answer:* To find out who "Amazing Grace" was and how she got her nickname 2. She thought it was important to help in the war effort and so she joined the women's branch of the Navy. 3. *Possible answer:* She worked with other mathematicians and engineers to develop modern computing machines for the Navy; 4. *Possible answer:* Today computers are important in almost every area of modern life, so she was right. **Word Work:** malfunction; launched; motto; mass; **Check:** B

**Tier 3, page 63: Read and Understand**: 1. *Possible answer:* To find out who "Amazing Grace" was and how she got her nickname 2. *Possible answer:* She was inquisitive, resourceful and determined to learn how things worked. 3. *Possible answer:* She worked with other mathematicians and engineers to develop modern computing machines for the Navy. 4. She dared to do things that girls in her day didn't normally do; she was brave, curious, hard-working, and always doing something. **Word Work:** *Sentences will vary; check students' work.* **Check:** B

## Two Poems

**Tier 1, page 66: Read and Understand**: 1. She is the gypsy queen that stands for October. 2. colorful autumn leaves 3. Everything looks red as the sun rises at daybreak, as if it were colored with a red crayon; 4. spring or summer because green apples aren't ripe yet in the poem; **Word Work:** could not; you are; she will; have not; **Check:** D

**Tier 2, page 67: Read and Understand**: 1. *Possible answer:* It makes October sound mysterious, grand, and like something that comes and goes. 2. Cold weather and wind weaken the plants, making them bend or "bow." 3. In each stanza, the 1st and 3rd lines don't rhyme, but the 2nd and 4th do; 4. sunny, misty, clear, still; **Word Work:** is; sleeps; are; stand; run; **Check:** D

**Tier 3, page 68: Read and Understand**: 1. *Possible answer:* It makes October sound mysterious, grand, and like something that comes and goes. 2. spring or summer because green apples aren't ripe yet; 3. The day has ended, and it's not a fresh new morning anymore. 4. Both use an ABCB pattern; lines in "October" are all about the same length, while the lines in "Green-Apple Morning" are long/short; **Word Work:** We arose early; You became strong; He bit an apple; Autumn winds blew; I caught the ball; **Check:** D

## Gliding Through the Air

**Tier 1, page 72: Read and Understand**: 1. Ted 2. He is scared but he has a sense of humor. 3. Ted is thinking them to himself; no 4. Not only was it Max's idea to take the flight, he also seems to be enjoying it. **Word Work:** quick-release, mechanism; non-powered, flight; stomach-churning, dips; sky-high, climbs; **Check:** A

**Tier 2, page 73: Read and Understand**: 1. *Possible answer:* He uses exaggeration, and jokes about what he sees and hears to get across how scared and anxious he is. 2. These show Ted's inner thoughts. He thinks them but doesn't say them aloud. 3. He pretends to have no real flying experience and he says that he needs luck to land safely. 4. He didn't want them to know how scared he really was, especially since Max wasn't. **Word Work:** E, D, A, B, C; **Check:** A

**Tier 3, page 74: Read and Understand**: 1. *Possible answer:* He uses exaggeration, wit, and irony to get across how scared and anxious he is. 2. They show Ted's inner thoughts. They show him to be skeptical and funny. 3. Captain Carl; he pretends to have no real flying experience and says that he needs luck to land safely. 4. His description of the flight was not nearly how he truly experienced it. **Word Work:** E, D, A, B, C; **Check:** D